W9-BYI-099

The Next Better Place

Also by
Michael C. Keith

Sounds in the Dark: All-Night Radio in American Life

Queer Airwaves: The Story of Gay and Lesbian Broadcasting
(with Phylis Johnson)

Talking Radio: An Oral History of American Radio in the Television Age

Waves of Rancor: Tuning In the Radical Right (with Robert Hilliard)

The Hidden Screen: Low-Power Television in America (with Robert Hilliard)

Voices in the Purple Haze: Underground Radio and the Sixties

Signals in the Air: Native Broadcasting in America

Global Broadcasting Systems (with Robert Hilliard)

The Radio Station

The Broadcast Century and Beyond: A Biography of American Broadcasting
(with Robert Hilliard)

Radio Programming: Consultancy and Formatics

Selling Radio Direct

Broadcast Voice Performance

Radio Production: Art and Science

Production in Format Radio Handbook

Dirty Discourse: Sex and Indecency in American Radio
(with Robert Hilliard)

The Next Better Place

A Father and Son
on the Road

by **Michael C. Keith**

**Algonquin Books
of Chapel Hill**

2003

Author's Note:
Some of the names of individuals and places have been invented
due to a failure of memory about specific events of my childhood.

Published by
Algonquin Books of Chapel Hill
Post Office Box 2225
Chapel Hill, North Carolina 27515-2225

a division of
Workman Publishing
708 Broadway
New York, New York 10003

Library of Congress Cataloging-in-Publication Data
Keith, Michael C., 1945–
    The next better place : a father and son on the road / by Michael C. Keith.
    p. cm.
    ISBN 1-56512-364-6
    1. Keith, Michael C., 1945—Childhood and youth.   2. Fathers and sons—
United States—Biography.   3. Children of alcoholics—United States—
Biography.   4. Hitchhiking—United States.   I. Title.
HQ755.85 .K444 2003
306.874'2—dc21   2002074509

10   9   8   7   6   5   4   3   2   1
First Edition

For my daughter, Marlo, and her papa . . .
wherever he might be.

Acknowledgments

Next to my family and some very
dear friends, the people most
responsible for seeing this book into
print are Christi Cardenas of the
Lazear Agency and Amy Gash of
Algonquin Books. Without their
expertise, guidance, and passion, one
of my fondest dreams would likely
have remained unrealized. Can you
imagine how difficult it is to repay
such an enormous debt?

Contents

Preface

At dinner with friends a few years ago, the conversation turned to the subject of childhood memories. Most of the accounts had to do with joyful events, family outings, and holidays. Occasional stories about the loss of a grandparent or a pet were the exceptions. When it was my turn, I blurted out the first thing that came to mind.

"I didn't crap for nearly two years once," I declared.

"Now that's a heartwarming recollection," quipped someone.

"It's true," I responded, adding that when you don't eat . . .

"So you're saying that you were starved as a child?" interrupted the wife of a colleague.

"And you were kept in a windowless basement, right?" said her husband with a playful smirk.

"Just the opposite," I replied. "I was free to roam the wide-open spaces and go pretty much where I wanted. The problem was meals were often few and far between."

"And this was because? . . . "

Before long I was recounting life on the road with my father, including the fact that, despite my now being an academic of some distinction, I hardly ever attended school, missing some grades entirely and never reaching beyond the first weeks of high school.

"God, our childhoods were so boringly normal compared to yours," observed one friend.

"Don't complain," I answered. "Normal is pretty good when you're a kid."

That night sleep was slow in coming and when it did it was anything but restful. My dreams retraced the highways my father and I wandered in vain pursuit of our utopias.

Who was it that said a normal childhood is one not worth living? I'd like to tell that person a story.

In the third-class seat sat the journeying boy.

—Thomas Hardy

The Next Better Place

PART I
ALBANY TO PITTSBURGH
(472 Miles)

The Giveaway

IT IS 1959. My mother and father talk while I pilot my scooter along the cement paths that surround the New York State Capitol. Rising from the cracks in the pavement are puffy white dandelion balls, atomic bomb mushroom clouds, which I run over as part of my search-and-destroy mission to save the planet. It is late spring and the flowers and trees are in full dress. I am about to be transferred to the care of my father, and my mother is justifiably reluctant to consummate the exchange.

This is the second try, and as before she makes my father promise that I will be properly fed and sheltered.

"I wouldn't be doing this if it wasn't so hard to make ends meet, you know. On my waitress pay I can hardly feed the girls, and the apartment is so small. Besides, he wants to be with you," she says, and pain and guilt are mingled in her defeated expression.

The girls she refers to are my sisters, both slightly younger than me.

My mother lights a pencil-length Pall Mall off the tip of my father's half-spent Camel. Her fingers are bony and long, spiderlike, and they tremble when she is nervous. They are trembling now. When I breeze by on my scooter, my parents smile and wave solicitously. I may be eleven but I know the score. Boys should be with their father, and girls should be with their mother. A natural symmetry. I don't mind. In fact I love my father, even though I know he's kind of a bum. Besides, I am bored with the dull routine of life with my mother and sisters. Schoolwork and bed before sunset are just a couple of things I am not crazy about. Her obsession with cleanliness is another. So this is really my choice.

"You want to be with him, don't you?" observes my mother. Her frustration with my obvious lack of enthusiasm for the home life she works so hard to create is increasingly apparent. I seek the life of adventure, and with my father each day is certain to be different.

When I get within earshot I hear my mother's strained voice laying out the ground rules. For the first time she strikes me as almost pretty enough to be in the movies, but like me she is too skinny to have a real chance at stardom, I think. Movie actors have sculpted muscles and hourglass figures—qualities we lack. In truth I have more physical deficiencies than she does. A big nose and funny-shaped head are not assets in Hollywood. Still, despite all these marks against me, I figure that being in the movies some day is not an impossibility, especially since I am certain that I possess a talent for showbiz, as my father calls it.

"Don't drink! If you start hitting the bottle again, I'll take him back. Bars are no place for a child. He needs to have a bath once a week and his clothes and underwear need to be washed. School is important. Make sure he goes every day. If there's a problem, just bring him back, okay?"

My father nods in agreement, although I know my mother's words are lost on him. She knows this too but clings to the hope that he will do right by me—for once own up to his responsibility and in doing so relieve her of the terrible burden she has borne since marrying him. He has never been any help to her or the kids because of his constant drinking, she is quick to tell anyone with a sympathetic ear.

"Don't worry. I'll take care of the kid. For Christ's sake, he's my son, too," says my father, feigning indignation by shaking his head and exhaling a glob of smoke from his broad nostrils.

"I wouldn't be doing this if I could afford to feed all three and give him someplace to sleep besides the sofa. He's too old to sleep in with his sisters. It wouldn't be right," says my mother, as if she were speaking to some invisible jury. "I swear to God, if you start boozing, I'll come and get him and that will be the end of it. You'll never have him again. Really, don't try anything. I'll call the cops. I mean it."

"Oh, pipe down, will you? You're not going to call anyone. You're full of crap! Jesus, I said I'd take care of him and I will! My back was killing me before. That's why I took a drink. To relieve the pain. It hasn't been right since the jeep accident. I got pills now. Let's not make a damn federal case out of it," responds my father as he lights a fresh cigarette with the stub of another.

My father's now almost mythical account of his army-related accident involves a jeep flipping over in the Aleutian Islands during World War II. This fabled mishap is responsible for his recurring back problems, he contends. My mother is skeptical about his whole account and at times tells him so.

"You weren't in the war. You never left the country. You typed supply reports at Fort Devens in Massachusetts. Remember? That's what you told me once."

"Like hell I did! What do you know about it? You think you have all the details?" he counters, pulling his cherished discharge from his wallet and waving it in her face. "You think they just give these away for the hell of it? You have to earn an *honorable* discharge."

I am intrigued by another of my father's physical abnormalities. His right-hand index finger—another casualty of his alleged army accident—is slightly misshapen and on top of that it is turning yellow. Weeks earlier when I asked him why it had changed color, he explained that it meant he would soon find a suitcase full of sawbucks. When I inquired as to why it hadn't turned green instead, he shrugged his shoulders, lifted his left leg, and farted loudly.

In the old days in Paris a man became a cabaret star because he could string farts together into a patriotic tune, kind of like "Yankee Doodle Dandy," but in froggy, my father likes to say. Whenever I envision this, it makes me laugh, sometimes hysterically. So far my father's been able to do up to four notes of "Blue Gardenia," one of his favorite Nat King Cole songs.

My mother calls out to me as I'm about to eradicate another row of radioactive weeds secretly planted by the Commies. It is time to conclude the deal and make our official farewells. She kisses me on the cheek and I rocket away as quickly as I can. Something inside causes me to withhold affection from her, and this will not change until we are both much older and I am a lot wiser. For much of our relationship there will be a point beyond which I will not go with her. A hug but not a kiss. An exchange of verbal affection that leaves her unfulfilled and wanting because I will not return her gestures of love. Maybe it is because I feel she is giving me away.

The huge weeping willow trees on the capitol lawn are absolutely still. Their drooping limbs remind me of the hanging cattle rustlers I saw in an episode of *Wagon Train*.

"Head 'em out," I whisper as my mother extends her sinewy arm in my direction.

"Love you, Michael!" she blurts out, nearly choking on a gulp of wind that has suddenly swooped down like a winged predator from the cold gray parapets of the capitol edifice and into her gaping mouth.

"Love yo—!"

Hitting the Road

IT HAS BEEN TWO YEARS since my parents divorced. I know this because when my mother is angry at my father or about her life in general, which is most of the time, she often says that she should have divorced him long before that. In fact she says she never should have married him in the first place, adding that you do stupid things when you're young and naive.

"At nineteen what do you know about people like him? I was a dumb little virgin, for heaven's sake!" she mutters while scrubbing clothes against a washboard in the kitchen sink, which is held upright by two rusted and bowed metal columns that stand at perilous angles to one another on a faded and stained linoleum floor. I think of them as firehouse poles or escape ramps for the cockroaches that climb from the mysterious recesses of the drain.

My father blames her for their failed relationship, claiming that his drinking wasn't the real problem but never saying what the real problem was. His bitterness over the divorce is never more apparent than when he is tipping the bottle. But now he has sworn to stay sober because of me. We have plans. For months we have talked about going to California, a place so beautiful, according to my father, that it makes Albany look like a piece of used toilet paper. He has never actually been there himself, but he knows people who have and they rave about it, he reports. So the West beckons, and I am dizzy with anticipation. Visions of rugged, snowcapped mountains, sunbaked deserts, famous movie stars, and towering palm trees fill my daydreams. I want to be there more than anything. My need to go is consuming me.

My father has a few things to take care of before we leave, he says, so I occupy my days running my scooter through the busy downtown streets near the rooming house where we are staying. To my delight but not surprise, my father has not pressed the issue of school, although he tells me to stay close by so that I won't be spotted by the truant officer. My mother knows nothing about our plans to leave Albany and I wonder how severely she will react when she finds out that we are gone. Will she have regrets for giving up her eldest child and only son? Do mothers care more about their female children? Will she really get the police after us to get me back? These are questions that are never too far from my thoughts.

It has been a year since my first abbreviated stay with my father, which ended when my mother caught sight of him coming out of a bar around the corner from the DeWitt Clinton Hotel, his occasional employer. He contends that she was spying on him and jumped to the wrong conclusion. He wasn't drinking, he protests, but simply looking for a friend from work, another bellhop. I know better too.

That night I am back in the damp basement flat on Hudson Avenue with my mother and two sisters, and it is at least a month before he is able to get back into the semigood graces of the woman he refers to as "that goddamn hardheaded mick" when he is unhappy with her. His language for her father, whom he hates and fears, is more choice. My grandpa Mac, short for McKenna, has threatened to beat the malarkey out of my father if he catches him drunk around us, and his reputation as a two-fisted brawler in his hometown adds considerable weight to his threat.

"Daddy will come up to Albany and straighten you out, mister," I recall my mother telling my father on more than one occasion to warn him off another round with the bottle.

"Straighten me out? Bullshit! He's the biggest friggin' drunken harp in Hartford," is my father's standard reply. "Don't tell me about that son of a bitch. You forget that he was such a lush that you and your sister ended up in an orphanage."

I have a vague memory of visiting my grandfather in a VA hospital when I was very young, and years later when I bring it up to my father he says, "The dumb bastard was in there drying out. Nearly killed himself drinking rubbing alcohol and Sterno."

Now on our first evening together my father cooks us Campbell's pork and beans on a single-burner hot plate and we discuss our planned trek to California, where he has a pal who works at a motel in a place called Encino and is certain to find a job for him.

"There's always work in the hotel racket," he says, adding, "I'll be glad to get out of this stinking jerk burg. Nothing but lousy luck for me here. I want to get as far away from the East Coast as I can. Leave all the crap behind. The farther the better, believe me."

Bitterness transforms his expression.

A couple of days later we are ready to hit the road, as my father puts it. We board a Greyhound bus to New York City after successfully eluding the rooming-house landlord, to whom my father owes back rent. Our departure means leaving behind my beloved scooter, salvaged from a junk pile in an alley behind the DeWitt Clinton. My father spotted it during a smoke break in his bellhop job and he and his buddy tightened a few screws, unbent the handlebars, scraped off some rust and grime, and hosed it down to get it presentable and in working order. After that he hauled it to my mother's flat, where I was staying at the time, and presented it to me with great fanfare as my sisters looked on with awe and envy. They were seldom recipients of attention let alone gifts from my father. I felt sorry for them but was pleased to be the chosen one.

Nothing in my life has meant as much to me as this recycled scooter. It gave me mechanized movement, a means to reach limits far beyond what my feet could provide. I was thrilled by the speed it could achieve and the ground it could cover. In my active imagination, the small rubber wheels took me to faraway, beautiful places.

Yet when the time came, I was more than willing to suffer the loss of my prized vehicle for the greater pleasures of a legitimate long-distance voyage.

At the Port Authority Bus Terminal in New York we are approached by a drunk clutching his crotch who asks my father directions to the "pissery," and it dawns on me that he is asking for the location of the bathroom. I adopt the term until my father warns me against using it, although I can't imagine that it is worse than the term my father mostly uses—*the crapper.*

"It's a swear word, so don't use it. I don't want you picking up language like that, okay?"

I agree but file it away for future use when he is not within earshot. The enormity of the bus station thrills me but the sensation is extinguished when my father tells me that we're too short of cash to catch the next bus. But this won't be a problem, he promises, because he has an old friend in town who can help out. He's not quite sure of his address, so he looks in a phone book that hangs from a cord at the end of a group of telephone booths.

"Not far from here. An easy walk," he announces.

Out on the street, the skyscrapers capture my attention.

"Some place," my father says proprietarily. "It's changed, though, since I was a kid. Not such a great burg anymore. Too bad."

I can see by the look in his grayish yellow eyes that for an instant he has been transported back to when it was a better place. He was born in a part of Harlem that was a middle-class white neighborhood in the early decades of the century.

"City has gone to the dogs." He is back and staring disdainfully at a JOHN F. KENNEDY FOR PRESIDENT poster attached to the wall of what appears to be an abandoned building.

He hates JFK because he is Irish, like my grandpa, and because Kennedy senior was a rum-running mick who bought his son's elections and whatever else he wanted, he claims.

"Without all their dirty money they couldn't get elected dogcatcher. Nixon came from poor parents, who couldn't afford to buy their kids into Harvard. They were decent people. Not crooks," contends my father, shaking his head indignantly.

To me Kennedy looks like a movie star, so I like him no matter what my father says. I have never seen a person with such white teeth, and maybe that is the real reason why my father hates him, because his own choppers are almost all rotted away and he has stained false ones for the top of his mouth.

"Come on, let's go to the square. You'll like that."

We join the fast-moving crowd as it defies the flashing DON'T WALK sign on the opposite side of the street. When we're about halfway across, a cab driver leans on his horn and shouts at us to move our fat asses, and my father thumbs his nose at him. That gesture nearly gets us run over. The sour smell of car exhaust is joined by a more pleasant odor coming from an umbrellaed hot dog cart that we nearly collide with while trying to escape the bumper of the Checker taxi.

"Son of a bitch!" shouts my father at the cab as it barrels away.

No one else seems quite as perturbed by the attempted homicide as he does. In fact I'm struck by the nonchalance of our fellow pedestrians, who also had to leap for their lives.

"Prick," grumbles my father under his breath as he tugs me deeper into the cement canyon that leads to his fabled square, a place that he has spoken about with considerable enthusiasm and longing for as long as I can remember.

Street Scenes

MY MOTHER HAS A TOASTER, but only one of its coils works, so our toast is always soft and cool on one side. It is better than the toast made on a tiny hot plate in my father's room back in Albany. It cooks unevenly and catches fire occasionally. When this happens, my father chucks the toast into the nearby sink and stamps out the flame with a dirty dish towel. This upsets me, since we usually pee in the sink during the night because the communal bathroom is at the far end of an unlit hallway.

"It's all right," he assures me while scraping off the singed areas and applying some colorless oleomargarine to what remains.

"Eat it," he orders. "It's better than nothing."

I'm not sure it is, but I do as he says. By the time we reach the periphery of the square, I am totally ravenous. The incinerated toast I swallowed for breakfast has completely left me.

"I'm starving," I complain, rubbing my growling stomach.

"So what's new?" says my father, checking his pockets.

After digging around a minute, he comes up with a couple of wrinkled dollar bills and some change. We stop at a hot dog stand that looks identical to the one we nearly banged into and I load my narrow bun with everything that is available until the mound I form is close to toppling.

"You ain't gonna taste da dog unner all dat crap, kid," comments the vendor as he hands my father a cup of coffee. That is his lunch. That and a Camel cigarette.

People stream by in thick columns, oblivious to our presence. One of these zombielike passersby bumps my father's arm as he is about to take a sip of his coffee, and the contents of the paper cup splatter onto his shirt. This sets him off, but before he has a chance to single out the culprit and give him a tongue-lashing, the assailant has melted back into the stream of bodies.

"Son of a bitch," growls my father, whose cigarette also falls victim to the crash.

His attempt to relight it fails, and this fans his anger. The cigarette is drenched beyond redemption and he heaves it to the ground. He mutters a few more profanities as he fetches another from his pack and lights it up. A long drag has the immediate effect of improving his mood.

"How's the hot dog?" he asks, and I offer him the last bite. "You eat it," he says with a wink, and we move toward the great square.

As we walk along he dabs at the splattered coffee marks on his shirt and asks if I can see the stains. When I nod that I can, he curses all New Yorkers and flicks the tiny remains of his lit cigarette into a trash can. His clothing is something he cares about, especially since he has only one other outfit.

"I hope the whole fucking city burns down," he grumbles, and then directs my attention to a mammoth smoking billboard that blows perfect rings.

"So what do you think?" he says, sweeping his hand grandly from left to right. "Times Square. It's something, huh?"

There are more signs and neon lights than I have ever seen in one place, and they have a hypnotic effect on me. My father is halfway down the block before I realize it, and I run to catch up to him.

"Stay with me," instructs my father. "You get lost here, I'll never find you."

We join a crowd that has gathered at the window of an Italian restaurant. Beyond the glass a man in a white apron and tall, puffy chef's hat is kneading a large mound of spongy dough. We are not sure why the crowd has formed to observe this mundane scene until the man tosses the stretched dough toward the ceiling and it lands on the counter in the form of an air-filled dome. The crowd laughs at this and becomes nearly uproarious when the pizza man pinches a small nipple into the top of the bulbous and quivering mound.

I am slow to catch on until a teenager with a carefully sculpted duck's-ass haircut next to me says, "Like to find a broad with a tit that big," while cupping his hands against his black leather jacket.

A few members of the crowd overhear him and snicker. My father signals for us to move away. There is a sheepish grin on his face and I make a point of letting him know that I am aware of the joke by cupping my hands across my chest like the teenager.

"Don't be smart," he warns, slapping at my hands, and we leave the spectacle behind.

Our next stop is a drugstore just around the corner. My father needs a pack of butts and I request a roll of Necco wafers. There is just enough money left to cover this purchase, and I sense that his old pal is crucial to our plans to reach California. As I wait for him in the entranceway, a tiny woman wrapped from head to foot in a soiled and tattered shawl approaches me and says that her son is the president of the United States. When I say, "Eisenhower?" she looks at me like I am a total idiot.

"No, Lincoln . . . Abraham Lincoln," she shouts, and wanders away in utter disgust.

When I report the encounter to my father, he says in a matter-of-fact manner that everybody in New York thinks they are either famous or related to somebody who is. I chew on this observation and a chocolate Necco wafer as we begin our movement up the rungs of Manhattan's teeming streets.

Twelve Steps

THE SO-CALLED EASY WALK to my father's friend's place turns out to be a considerable journey. I count forty-seven blocks, and the old man (that is how I think of him at times like these) is huffing and puffing. His new pack of cigarettes is half emptied along the way, and when he exhales smoke it is accompanied by a whirring sound that puts me in mind of the air-raid sirens in movies about the bombing of London. When I tell him this, he claims it has nothing to do with his smoking. That it's a combination of bronchitis and asthma and I should learn to be more sensitive to what ails him. Baloney, I think, but I don't say so.

We take a right off Broadway at Eighty-eighth Street and find the Oxford Arms Hotel and Apartments a half block later. It is twelve stories high—I carefully note the number of floors—and it has a faded brown awning extending over its entrance. I am impressed and my father's expression indicates he is too.

We pass through a revolving door, which I speed up in an attempt to catch the heels of my father's shoes. He shoots me a "cut the crap" look as we enter a sparsely furnished lobby housing two anemic-looking potted palms. At the far end, in a room behind a wall of glass, a dozen or so men are intently listening to a speaker, who stands behind a podium bearing a crest of crossed sabers. Even from our distant vantage point it is apparent that the speaker is emaciated and unsteady. He stabs at his brow with a plaid handkerchief and at one point leans so far to one side that he seems about to crash to the floor. Someone quickly takes up a position a few feet behind him as if ready to catch him should he tip over. A sign to the left of the door leading into the room says TWELVE-STEP MEETING—WELCOME.

At the hotel desk, a colored man, who to me is the spitting image of Nat King Cole, greets us. My father tells him we are here to see his friend Ray Scanlon.

"He be right behind you, sir," the desk clerk responds, pointing a long finger that reminds me of a White Owl cigar toward a heavy-set figure approaching us from the direction of the meeting room.

"Curt, you ole bastard!" Ray shouts. "You mean you're still alive? Jesus, I thought the devil would've claimed your nasty ass by now."

My father is obviously pleased by his friend's enthusiastic greeting. They shake hands vigorously and launch into a conversation about life over the past several years. I return my attention to the frail-looking speaker in the twelve-step room, who has just completed his talk and is smiling tentatively and nodding at the applauding audience. Moving toward the room, I can discern a distinct lack of color in his narrow face and eyes so deeply set in their sockets that I wonder if he sees everything as if from the dark depths of a cave.

"Michael, come meet Mr. Scanlon," says my father, and I return to his side.

"Ray . . . call me Ray, buddy," he says, and takes my skinny fingers into his meaty fist and playfully swings my arm in circles as if it were a rubber band.

"Well, the kid lucked out, Curt. Got his mom's good looks and not your ugly puss. Wouldn't have wished that beak on my mother-in-law. So you're Mikey, eh? You're a pretty tough lookin' little guy."

Ray's warm and robust manner appeals to me immediately, and I like him because he teases my father without really putting him down.

"Curt, you're just in time for a little AA reinforcement," he says, nodding in the direction of the meeting still under way. "So how long you been on the wagon, pal?"

My father lies, saying that he has been without a drink going on three years. In reality it has been less than three months, and that is something of a record for him.

The memory of his most recent bout with the bottle is still all too vivid to me: He is stumbling down the steps that lead to my mother's basement apartment. She instructs my sisters and me to remain perfectly still until he leaves, because she is not about to open the door and deal with him, especially now that they are officially divorced.

We huddle behind the door and listen while he pounds on it and shouts for my mother to let him in. He uses lots of swear words and threatens to kick the door down, adding that he will also kick my mother's bony Irish ass when he gets in. Eventually he gives up and leaves, or so we think. When my mother believes the coast is clear she opens the door, only to discover that he is sprawled out on the steps. With the help of her friend Peggy Phelps, who lives on the floor above, she manages to get him to his feet and back onto the sidewalk, where he wanders off in his alcohol-induced stupor.

A couple of days later he returns, but this time he appears sober or close to it. My mother is not interested in his apologies and tells him so through the opening in the chained door. Despite his dramatic pleas that he be allowed to visit with me and my sisters, she refuses to let him into the apartment.

"You think I'm going to let you in after all the threats you made the other day? Besides, I don't want the kids to see you like this. You're pathetic. Look at you. You're shaking like a spastic. They're just babies. Is this the way you want them to see their father? Don't you know what you've done to this family already? You've ruined things. You've always just thought of yourself. Not us. Never, never us. Just leave."

With these words she closes the door in his face. Tears well up in her vast green eyes, and they run down my cheeks in torrents. My sisters are whimpering as they back themselves into a dark corner of the living room. There they remain until my mother assures them that everything is all right, and then and only then do they emerge from their sanctuary like frightened lambs treading cautiously lest they arouse a sleeping bogeyman. Sadness overwhelms me when I think of my father standing dejected on the other side of the door. This image makes me cry all over again. If I had the power to make things better, I would in an instant. But I am powerless against his raging thirst.

Gert's Loss

"SO WHAT BRINGS YOU to the city?" asks Ray.

My father explains that the hotel racket, as he calls it, in Albany is flat on its ass, so we're heading to the West Coast, where he has a good lead on a job. But right now dough is low, he says, and he wonders if Ray can help out.

Ray says he will do what he can but that things are not great for him either, not since the death of his daughter last year. After that, he says, his wife became pretty weird, and he has been too distracted by the situation to put in the hours he needs to make a decent living. Managing the Oxford Arms has been difficult in his current state of mind, he says, and his expression loses its animation.

"Poor Gert. She's been off her lid. Strange as hell. Not that it wasn't hard on me. I was crushed and still am. Katy was the light of my life. When she died it seemed like everything kind of went dark. We did everything together. The pain is still there, believe me, but I'm trying to get on with things. Gert's just thrown in the towel."

My father conveys his sympathies, and Ray suggests that he do some things at the Oxford to make a few bucks. He agrees, and I am not too happy because this means a delay in our travel plans. I just want to get going again, to board a bus west. There is no offer of cash from Ray, so our wheels are locked in place for the time being. Shit! I scream to myself, wishing the whole world could hear me.

"Just a few days, then we'll have enough dough to get a ticket," my father assures me later, but his words do little to raise my spirits.

Ray tells my father that he can bunk in a small room off the lobby that is usually used to store luggage and things, while I stay with him and his wife. I am not at all pleased with this arrangement and give my father a look that says so. He is not happy with it either but signals me to keep my mouth shut. All the warning alarms are sounding inside my head. This is not good. Not good at all.

"It'll probably be nice for Gert to have a kid around," observes Ray, who then tells my father about an AA meeting that evening in what he calls the Sobriety Lounge.

"We got meetings every day, sometimes two," points out Ray, and my father says, "Great," but I know he's really thinking something else, as he does not have much use for AA.

Ray nods in the direction of the glassed-in room, whose current occupants are huddled around a table piled with white mugs and a coffee urn, and then he introduces us to Leland, his desk clerk, whom he instructs to show my father to his accommodations. Leland is humming "Nature Boy," and when I look at him he flashes me a smile that reveals a large dark gap between his gleaming front teeth. Ray and I head to the elevator that will take us to his apartment, and it feels like the long walk to the electric chair.

"Don't be a nuisance," says my father as we move in opposite directions.

"Hey, if he is, I'll give him a good one," jokes Ray, holding his clenched fist above my head.

Inside the elevator, Ray asks if I have ever been to Coney Island, and I tell him no. He says it has rides that make even grown-ups soil their pants, and he wants to know if I want to go. I am keen on the idea and tell him so. The last time I was at an amusement park was with my father when I was nine years old. He was drinking and I managed to talk him into riding the roller coaster with me. When the ride ended, he was not feeling too well and threw up all over his recently purchased Hush Puppies. For the balance of the day he tried in vain to get all of the puke off his shoes while cursing me for getting him to go on the ride in the first place. The incident seemed to me to be a form of retribution for his alcohol abuse, and I was secretly pleased that he got what he deserved. Maybe he would stop drinking if he got sick from it, I thought.

"These Hush Puppies are new. Now look at them. They ought to close down that goddamn ride," he complained, digging vomit particles out from his treasured shoes with the tip of his Ace comb.

"It's the beer," I countered, to which he responded by chucking the befouled comb at me.

The elevator stops at the eleventh floor and we enter a carpeted hallway. At the far end an elderly woman is forcing a box into an opening in the wall. When Ray catches sight of her, he comments to me that she puts things into the incinerator that would not burn if they were dropped into an active volcano. He says that he would like to stuff her down the chute and would if the old bag was not so punctual with her rent money.

On the door to his apartment, a wide black ribbon hangs under a sign that says THE SCANLONS. This gives me the shivers and I am filled with trepidation as we enter. I think of my father in his cozy storage room miles beneath me as I am escorted into the lair of a crazy woman.

Unwelcome Guest

MRS. SCANLON GLARES AT ME. There is a look in her eyes that says she'll get me if it's the last thing she ever does. Her black hair is wound tightly into a large cone atop her head, which makes her appear all the more threatening and evil. For a moment Ray says nothing, as if calculating his next move. The living room is dark except for the flickering glow emanating from a silent television screen. Ray removes his hand from my shoulder and moves to his wife's side. There they stand looking at me, and I wonder if the ghost of their daughter will hate me too for being there.

"He looks a little like Katy, doesn't he, Gert?" says Ray in a conciliatory tone.

Mrs. Scanlon shoots him a look of ferocious contempt and stomps away. Ray shrugs his shoulders and exhales loudly as if he has been holding his breath.

"Mikey is going to stay with us for a while," he announces as his wife slams the door to the room she has entered.

Ray points out that she is not herself and then says I can stay in Katy's room. The idea fills me with absolute dread. I cannot imagine sleeping in a dead person's bed. It would be like nestling in the arms of a corpse or being cuddled by something cold and vile. Ray rejects my offer to bunk on the couch and leads me to his daughter's room. On the way to this tomb I begin to plot my escape. I will slip out later and get my father. We can get help someplace else, I reason. To hell with this arrangement.

The bedroom is as dark as a crypt and I sense the little dead girl's presence, but when the light is turned on it seems much less foreboding. There are brightly colored stuffed animals piled on the bed and in a rocking chair that is covered with a patchwork quilt. The curtains and rug are a welcoming sunshine yellow. I figure that it might be safe to stay in the room as long as the light remains on. As soon as I am left alone, I plan to push the dresser in front of the closet door because my instincts tell me that Katy is in there waiting to exact her revenge on me for trespassing.

"She loved this thing," says Ray, lifting a Hula-Hoop and placing it over my head and around my waist. "Got it a few months before she passed on. Could keep it going for a long time, but toward the end she didn't have the energy. How about you? Any good at it?" he asks, but before I can answer he lets the hoop drop to the floor and moves away.

The longer we are in the room the more solemn he becomes. When his gloom hits bottom he abruptly turns and heads to the door, leaving me standing in front of a picture of his deceased daughter. I cannot detect any similarity in our looks, other than the fact that we both have thick brown hair, and lips that have too much red in them, at least to my liking. Grown-ups have commented about my ruby-colored lips, saying they look like they belong on a girl. It angers and upsets me when I hear this, so when I remember to do it, I pinch my lips together to draw the blood from them. For a second or so after I do this I look more masculine, I think.

"There's some good bologna and milk in the icebox. Help yourself," advises Ray at the door. He tells me to make myself at home and to hit the hay soon because I will need my rest for tomorrow when we go to Coney Island.

"You can't be groggy on the Parachute Drop if you want to stay alive," he warns.

On his way out of the apartment, he encounters his wife. There is a heated exchange and I can hear most of what is said. Mrs. Scanlon wants to know why he has brought me to their apartment. She calls me a dirty little orphan and demands that I be removed from the premises straightaway. She says Ray has no right putting some disgusting street urchin in their beloved daughter's room, that by doing so he is violating her memory. I resolve to vanish in the middle of the night.

The argument continues unabated for several minutes. Mrs. Scanlon does most of the talking. Finally Ray promises that I will be gone in a day or two, but this does little to appease his wife. As a further concession he tells her that I will sleep on the living room couch, which is fine by me and was my idea in the first place. This seems to have a positive effect on Mrs. Scanlon. When he returns to his daughter's bedroom, his face is flushed as if he has been hanging from his feet.

"Hey, buddy, sorry about all the racket. How about camping out on the couch tonight? You can watch TV until you fall asleep. We leave it on all the time these days. There are some good westerns on tonight," he says, attempting to conceal the anger and embarrassment he is feeling.

He fetches a blanket and pillow from a hall closet and tells me to use the blue guest towel in the bathroom, not the yellow ones, which belong to Katy. He says he will see me after the AA meeting and tells me to live it up and not worry about Gert, who will come around, he says. The fear I felt at the prospect of sleeping in the dead girl's bed is supplanted by the fear of being left alone in the apartment with Mrs. Scanlon. Will she come after me as soon as her husband leaves? Is she insane? Did she kill her own daughter? A monster begins to take shape in my distressed mind.

Ray cannot be sold on the idea of my accompanying him to the Sobriety Lounge, so as soon as he departs I take up a position on the couch that gives me a clear view of the door behind which Mrs. Scanlon patiently awaits the right moment to avenge my unwanted presence.

For as long as I can, I alternate my gaze between the door and the figures on the television screen, who ride their quick palominos across the landscape of my dreams.

Apparitions

"COWBOYS DON'T DIE . . . only Indians," declares my youngest sister, Pamela.

She looks like a miniature Dale Evans in her rhinestone blouse, leather jodhpurs, and white Stetson hat. We are leaning against the fence in a corral filled with magnificent black horses. They are wild, unbroken. The dream of motion is in their eyes, as it is in mine, and I can tell they desperately want to run free, to escape the world of humans. The wind stirs the dust and for a moment the horses are lost in a brown vortex. The frantic sound of their hooves is the only evidence of their existence. When the air settles I see my sister astride the largest and fiercest of the ebony stallions. I am filled with a combination of envy and horror.

My mother screeches an incomprehensible string of words from inside the barn as the animal carrying my sister jumps over the fence. Her small body is catapulted into the air and returns to earth behind a large cluster of sagebrush. I dash over to where I estimate she has landed, and when I get there my sister and father are lighting Camel cigarettes. My father asks if I want a butt, and they both begin to laugh wildly. I wake up full of confused anger.

The apartment is dark, but someone is in the kitchen making a considerable amount of noise. As I slowly survey my surroundings, I see Mrs. Scanlon sitting motionless across the room. Her eyes are fixed on me. My heart starts to pound and I feel small, warm droplets slip from my bladder into my undershorts. At any moment I expect her to fly across the room like a vampire bat and seize me, ripping at my gullet until a geyser of blood gushes from it. Before I can decide on a course of action, she dabs at the corner of her eyes with a tissue and retreats to her room, gently closing the door behind her.

Ray emerges from the kitchen with an apron wrapped around his thick midsection. He asks if I'm going to sleep all day and waves for me to join him in the kitchen, where I am introduced to a steaming pile of pancakes and a pitcher of orange juice.

"You're awfully scrawny. Bet you don't weigh much more than Katy did, and she was a little feather. But you're a guy and need some meat on those bones. Don't your old man feed you?" he asks, loading my plate.

I ask Ray about my father and am told that he has been put to work to raise the money we need to continue our passage west. This pleases me, and the dark clouds are momentarily pushed aside. The urgency that I feel to get to that golden destination has not diminished. If anything it has increased. It occupies the largest place in my thoughts and it is all I really care about now. My mother and sisters exist in there somewhere, but aside from in my dreams, they are inconsequential shadows on the sun-drenched plains of my westbound fixation.

At the table Ray asks if his wife has said anything to me, and I report that she has not. She will come around, he promises again, and flops another pancake on my emptied plate.

After breakfast I douse my hair with Ray's Vitalis, make a pass at my teeth with my index finger and a dot of toothpaste from a half-used tube of Gleem, and join him in the hall outside the apartment, where he is having an animated conversation with the old woman from the incinerator chute. This time she is attempting to squeeze a tattered sofa pillow half the size of her body into the narrow opening.

When we are on the elevator, Ray curses her and repeats his threat to shove her down what he calls the hole to hell. But his mood brightens when he begins outlining our day's itinerary. We are off to Coney Island, but first, he says, we must stop to pick up a couple of teenage boys who work for him part-time. He has promised them a day at the amusement park as well. A sort of bonus for them. I am not happy that there will be others with us, especially some older kids.

As we climb into his shiny green-and-white Chevy Bel Air, I feel a little pang of guilt about leaving my father behind to toil while I head off for a day of fun. Amusement parks are not an appealing form of diversion for him, I remind myself, recalling what I now regard as Hush Puppies Puke Day.

As the car is rolling up the alley, Ray pats me on the head and remarks that I have the same shape mouth as his daughter, at least the same ruby-colored lips. He pulls a photo from his wallet to prove his point, but I remember the picture on her dresser well enough to know what he means.

"She was a good girl. Loved the Hula-Hoop, but I already told you that, right?" he says, and then tucks the picture away as we enter the molten flow of traffic spilling across Eighty-eighth Street toward Broadway.

Undertows and Rub-a-Dub-Dubs

ON THE WAY to pick up Ray's teenage employees, Rick and Scooter, I learn that Katy died from a disease called leukemia. A form of cancer, says Ray. Before I can ask him for some details about the fatal affliction, he changes the subject, asking me if my mother knows where I am. Sure, I respond, and twist the facts further by stating that she and my sisters plan to join us once we are in California. He nods and remains silent the rest of the way.

The teens remind me of the young punks in the movie *The Blackboard Jungle*. When they see me they snicker and whisper something to each other. I know this does not bode well.

"Say hi to Mikey, like in 'take a hikey,'" says Ray, chuckling, and they mumble a greeting as they climb into the backseat of the Chevy.

Ray says a few words about how they will be cleaning an apartment at the Oxford this coming weekend that was just vacated by a tenant who kept a pet goat, but the boys are oblivious to his comment. Conceding this, Ray responds by turning on the radio. This gesture they respond to by asking him to raise the volume.

We weave our way through the dense city traffic toward Coney Island to the accompaniment of blaring rock 'n' roll music. This strikes me as pretty cool until one of the teenagers snaps the back of my head with his finger. I turn and give him a hard look, but this only inspires a loud, mocking burp from him and an eruption of laughter from his partner. I would like to beat up both of them in front of an admiring and cheering crowd in Tombstone or Yuma—someplace where avenging the vile deeds of young gunslingers wins a person a deputy sheriff's badge and the everlasting appreciation of timid townsfolk. To enhance this image I quietly whistle the theme from the movie *High Noon,* one of my favorite westerns.

Over the years, I have developed a substantial repertoire of movie music that I invoke in appropriate situations. My list of most popular themes also includes music from the movies *Picnic* with William Holden and Kim Novak, *The Bridge on the River Kwai* with Alec Guinness, *The Guns of Navarone* with Gregory Peck, and *The Magnificent Seven* with Yul Brynner. I've been using the latter theme song since we started our trip because it is the best western movie music I have ever heard, and when I shut my eyes I can see the seven heroic cowboys galloping across the spectacular desert to do battle with wicked desperadoes. They will right the wrongs of these horrible men and restore goodness to the world. My father loves "As Time Goes By" from *Casablanca,* but when he whistles or hums it a lot it usually means that he is going to start drinking, so I counter with a less sad song in the hope of distracting him from the bottle.

As soon as we reach our destination, Rick and Scooter suggest we all go for a dunk before doing anything else, so we jog toward the beach. I explain that I have no swim trunks and Ray says to use my underpants. The teens agree, commenting that nobody will care, but they have worn their swim trunks under their dungarees, as has Ray.

The idea of being in full view of thousands in my shorts does not appeal to me in the least, especially since they are pee stained. Instead I roll up my pant legs to just above my knees so that I can at least wade in the water. As I am standing on the ocean's edge, Scooter hoists me above his head like a surfboard and carries me out to a point that I calculate is deeper than I am tall. Ray is nowhere to be spotted as I demand to be returned to shore. Scooter remarks that I am as light as a noodle and adjusts his hold so that one of his hands is on the back of my neck and the other between my legs. He reports to Rick that I feel like I am missing some equipment or maybe I have a pussy instead of a dong, and they both laugh like stupid hyenas. Then he says my ass is like his little sister's, and he turns me sideways and pulls my pants halfway down to prove his point. His buddy concurs, squeezing my rear end with his clammy fingers.

My terror is replaced by mortification and rage. I manage to grab Scooter by the fins of his DA and pull at them with all my might, and he retaliates by heaving me into the water. I sink beneath the surface like a rock, all the while tugging at my pants and keeping my eyes open in the hope of finding something to grab hold of to keep from drowning. There is nothing to grasp, however, and I am more ashamed of not knowing how to swim than I am fearful of dying.

When someone takes me by the waist and hauls me to shore, I can only think to appear as nonchalant as possible so that Rick and Scooter will see that I am as tough as they are. But as soon as I am deposited onshore, tears gush from my burning eyes.

"You okay, pal?" asks Ray, who is my rescuer.

He does not seem to know what has transpired and advises me not to go out so far and to stay with Rick and Scooter because they are good swimmers and can keep an eye on me. As I am digging the sand out of my pockets, both teenagers appear and ask what has happened. Ray tells them that I am trying to drink the Atlantic, and they laugh and ask me if I'd like a wiener to go with it because they are on their way to the snack bar.

I sit on a boardwalk bench for a couple of hours while Ray and his teenage friends swim in the chilly surf. Later we all head to the public showers, where Ray insists I wash the sand and salt from my body and shake out my clothes before we start home. He does not want half of Coney Island in his car, he says, adding that we will come back and go on the rides another time because it is getting late and he has things to do. This only deepens my disappointment about the way things have turned out.

There are no individual shower stalls, just a row of showerheads mounted a few feet apart on a cement wall. By the time I get my damp clothes off, Scooter and Rick are lathering up and Ray is already patting dry his thick torso, having spent a few quick seconds under the spray.

"Here, sport, de-scum yourself," says Rick, flipping me a bar of soap, which bounces off my leg and into the sudsy puddle beneath my feet.

I begin to run the soap over my body when he grabs my arm and yanks the bar from my hand.

"Not like that, twerp! Hell, you're never gonna get the crud off that way, is he, Scooter?"

Of course his buddy agrees wholeheartedly, and they begin to scrub me with the soap, paying special attention to my backside. At intervals Scooter strokes his penis, which has begun to grow and rise. Ray is oblivious to my protests, and for what seems just short of an eternity four hands move over me until I am a virtual tepee of soapsuds.

"Hey, Ray, dig this. It's Frosty the Snowboy," quips Rick.

"Cut it out! He's clean enough, for Christ's sake," barks Ray, finally looking up as he wrestles with his socks.

Rick and Scooter, whose dong has returned to its normal size and elevation, leave the shower, and I quickly rinse off. Although I am facing the wall, I can tell that I am being observed, and when I leave the shower area I cover my privates, holding one hand over my genitals and the other over my rear end. This inspires a loud round of chuckling and Scooter starts to sing, "The shrimp boats are a-coming." Rick joins in, and the duo eyeball me as I throw on my clothes.

On the ride home I sit in back with Scooter while Rick rides up front with Ray. The car windows are open and the wind makes me shiver as it passes through my still-damp shirt and pants. I retreat to the protected environment of the floor rather than ask that the windows be closed. No one notices this up front since the passenger is dozing and the driver is lost in the music on the radio and the challenge of navigating the busy streets.

Scooter notices, however, saying that I look like I am turning blue. With that remark he shifts his body on the seat so that he is directly above me, and he puts his muscular legs around my shoulders, pinning me in place and forcing my face against his lap. I attempt to extricate myself from his hold but to no avail, and whenever I make a move to break his embrace he squeezes his legs so that I can barely catch my breath. It is like this all the way back to the Oxford Arms.

Only when Ray pulls the car into its alley parking space does Scooter loosen his grip. When he does I jump away from him, but not before administering a sharp blow to his thigh. He curses me under his breath and takes a swipe at me, but I am out of the car before he can make contact.

Nat King Cole

LELAND IS AT the check-in desk. He has a blue bandana wrapped tightly around his hair, which reminds me of Aunt Jemima on the syrup bottle, and he is writing something in a checkered notebook. When I ask about my father he says ole Curt is in his room resting. Had a hard day. Did a lot of muscle work. I find this last statement amusing, considering that my father is just a taller version of my skinny self. His pants hang on his gaunt frame the way they do on mine.

Ray has gone to his apartment and has instructed me to follow shortly, as supper will be ready soon. I want to catch my father and convince him to leave this place as soon as possible, maybe tomorrow. There is no way I am going to deal with the young punks or crazy Mrs. Scanlon anymore. To hell with those queers and that nutty woman!

Leland smiles broadly and again I am reminded of my father's favorite crooner, as he calls him. Figuring that it can only flatter him, I ask Leland if he is any relation to Nat King Cole. His eyes beam and he is clearly pleased by the comparison.

"No, sonny, but sho wish I was. Could use a kinfolk with all that scratch. 'Sides, he be better lookin' than me or anybody in my butt-ugly family, that's fo' sho," he responds with a theatrical shake of his head, and the cavernous gap between his front teeth confirms his self-evaluation.

I tell him that I still think he could be Nat's twin brother and he says that I don't have very good eyes for someone of my tender age. But I sense he fancies himself the singer's look-alike and works at it too. When I turn to go to my father's room, he says that I remind him of the kid on that TV western whose daddy has that funny-looking stubby rifle, and then he tells me not to wake my father if he is sleeping. A man of his years needs his sack time, he says. This comment makes my father sound older than I think of him as being, and I wonder if he will be up to the long road ahead. Fifty-one is pretty ancient to me, so I figure he might have a heart attack or something else immobilizing from the exertion caused by the demands of westward travel. If he does, it will not stop me. I will keep going. Nothing is going to prevent my seeing California, I declare to myself.

His room is tiny and windowless and thick with cigarette smoke. He calls me Butch when I enter—it is his favorite nickname for me. I don't know where it comes from and neither does he when I question him about its origin.

"It's just one of those words that people use for their kids or pets," he explains.

He is sitting on the edge of a foldout cot in his soiled boxer shorts and a T-shirt that has yellow rings under the armpits. When he attempts to clear his throat, he has a coughing fit. In midhack he takes a deep drag on the stub of his cigarette and then dashes it out in a butt-filled tin container, like the ones Table Talk pies come in, which he is using as an ashtray.

"So what have you been up to?" he asks.

I notice a couple of small scratches and a clot of dried blood on the shin of his left leg. He follows the path of my eyes and reports that he bumped his leg while moving a sofa. Actually, he says, the sofa slipped from his hands while he and another guy were hauling it down a flight of stairs. Too damn big to fit in the elevator, he explains.

"Maybe you could have put it down the incinerator," I quip, and he looks at me like I'm a kook.

My father's hair is gray—actually more white than anything. In stark contrast, his bushy eyebrows are jet-black. They remind me of fuzzy awnings and I tease him about it. He keeps them that way with a Maybelline eyebrow pencil, which he usually takes great care to conceal. Not expecting any visitors, he has left it resting beside his Gillette razor and Ace comb on a small stand near his cot. On two occasions I have actually witnessed him applying the dark liner. He is not aware of my spying on him and I know he would be extremely embarrassed if his secret for maintaining his youth was revealed. Although soap would only make contact with his face if it was thrown at him, as my mother once remarked during one of their many battles, he maintains the appearance of his eyebrows with unwavering devotion. I plan to preserve this knowledge until it serves me to do otherwise. It is my high card, my super weapon should I ever need to zap him really good, but I know there are likely to be dire consequences of my doing this. He will not be happy that I know he is using girl makeup to hide the white hairs in his poofy eyebrows.

Our brown canvas bag sits on the only chair, a three-legged stool, in his room. It contains everything we own. We have left several things besides my scooter back at the Albany rooming house so as to make our unlawful departure as inconspicuous as possible. My father does not want a confrontation with the landlord, "a real miserable old bastard" is how he describes him. Our swift exit has left me with only a partial change of clothes, something that would displease my mother, who above all else insists on cleanliness. Besides the shower at the beach, I have not had a bath in quite a while, at least not since rejoining my father, and that is fine with me. His laissez-faire attitude about personal hygiene is one of the attractions of life with him. Neither one of us is particularly big on getting wet unnecessarily, and the events of the day serve to deepen my commitment to this ideal.

Following my account of Coney Island, excluding the parts about nearly drowning and being harassed by the teenage bullies, I launch into my appeal about leaving right away. To my surprise and relief my father agrees, saying that the work he is doing in this dump is backbreaking, which given his war injury can be perilous. However, he says tomorrow is too soon and we will have to stick it out another day or so until he can get a few bucks together.

I suggest that he borrow some money from Leland, but my father already knows the score there, commenting that the Oxford Arms desk clerk is supporting a houseful of relatives with his meager paycheck. I take this to mean that he has already broached the subject with him.

"He's a real good guy but poor as a church mouse. He gave me a pack of butts. Spends a lot of dough on his hair too. It costs a bundle to get it processed like that. Not easy to straighten that kinky wool out. That's why he keeps the snot rag around his head. So it don't all coil up again because of the heat and humidity. He gives everything else to his family. Got a great voice. Sounds just like Nat King Cole. He sang a little bit of 'Blue Gardenia' for me. I told him to go on that talent-scout show on TV and win a lot of money, but he doesn't think he's good enough. Doesn't have much confidence," says my father, who then mentions his own appearance as a young wanna-be crooner on a radio show broadcast from the Bond Hotel in downtown Hartford.

"They had me audition for this program that came from the piano lounge. A few days later they put me on because some banjo player got sick and couldn't perform. I wasn't bad either, considering I never had one voice lesson and couldn't read music. Should of stuck with it. Who knows, maybe I would have made it big," he says, clearing phlegm from his throat and spitting it into the tin ashtray.

"Hey, bet you never heard this on the radio. It was long before you were born," he says, cupping his hands into the shape of a megaphone and miming an ancient radio jingle:

> Tastyeast is tempting to your appetite.
> Creamy wholesome candy, try a luscious bite.

Vitamins are hiding in this candy bar;
Pep, vim, and vigor linger where they are.
Children like this lovely creamy food delight;
Let them eat it daily, every morning, noon, and night.

"That sounds dumb," I say, adding that I'm pretty good at crooning too.

"Yes, you are, Mario," he responds, making reference to my rendition of Mario Lanza's "Be My Love," which I perform for him every chance I get.

"Maybe you'll get on the radio someday like your old dad, but you've got to wait till you grow up and your voice matures. Now you sound a little squeaky on the high notes and a little high on the low notes."

When I protest that I sound just like Mario, he says that on the radio I would probably sound more like Shirley Temple.

This is not the first time we have had this conversation and the outcome is never to my liking, so to heck with him. I know in my heart I'll be on the radio someday, and besides, I am impatient to pin down our departure date. Again he says it will be a day or two before we can hit the road, so I turn to leave, feeling dissatisfied. On my way out of his room my father tells me not to take any wooden nickels, and this is followed by a series of convulsive coughs. As I slowly traipse down the hall to get the elevator to the Scanlons' floor, I can hear him mimicking my voice, but no sooner does he get "For no one else can end this yearning" out than he begins to hack violently and strain to clear his obstructed windpipe. Even at eleven years old I doubt a body can withstand so much trauma and continue to operate, but he will survive far longer than these horrible spasms would indicate.

Forty-second Street Aliens

THE NEXT DAY MARKS the first of June and it continues to be unseasonably warm. Hotter than a Hotpoint in hell, remarks Ray, whose plaid sport shirt is half tucked into his khaki Bermuda shorts. His summer wardrobe is highlighted by a pair of calf-high black army boots that he proudly claims were issued to him in World War II. I ask if he knew my father during the war.

"Didn't know your old man until after the war," he answers, and I tell him that my father was in a near-fatal jeep accident chasing some Japs on icy islands off Alaska.

"Damn! Japs in Alaska? Didn't know they made it up that far," remarks Ray, shaking his head.

"That's how he hurt his back," I continue. "He got an honorable discharge too. Keeps it in his wallet."

"Well, that's something," says Ray, appearing suitably impressed.

Our plans for the day include a trip to an air-conditioned theater to see a movie of my choice. Ray is taking another day off for mental health reasons, he says with a wink and a smile. My teenage antagonists are not invited. Also to my great relief is the absence of Mrs. Scanlon in the morning. The door to her room is tightly closed against the activities of the living world.

Before noon we are off to the subway. Ray is not bothering with his car because he says it is impossible to park it in the Theater District. My father is nowhere in sight and when I ask Ray about his whereabouts he says my old man is on latrine duty in apartment 257. Seeing that I do not understand, he adds that getting piss and poop stains out of porcelain is a challenging job. I get the picture and figure that this will probably put my father in the right frame of mind to want to set the wheels in motion for our getaway tomorrow. This thought heightens my spirits nearly to the boiling point. Finally the highway and the mystical Rocky Mountains and Painted Desert it leads to. These are places I have studied back home on my Rand McNally road map of the United States for the last several months in intense anticipation of this journey.

In the subway bound for Forty-second Street an old man wrapped in a torn and filthy overcoat and wearing newspapers for shoes is sprawled out on the seat next to us. He reeks of alcohol and has vomited on the floor beneath him. Each time the crowded train lurches, the pink-and-yellow puddle shifts, forcing us to lift our feet to avoid being hit by it. Intermittently, the snoozing drunk mumbles profanities, which everyone within earshot does his or her best to ignore, but it is not easy.

"Now there's a guy who could use an AA meeting," remarks Ray, poking me with his heavy elbow.

The first thing I notice when we surface from the train into Times Square is the exhaling billboard. I feel a certain connection with the smoky sign because of my father's loyal use of the product it advertises. Ray jokes that the guy inside blowing those rings all day must have a worse hack than my old man. I doubt it.

Forty-second Street, which I had only caught a glimpse of on our trek to the Oxford Arms, is an awesome sight. Moviegoing is my favorite activity, so to behold a dozen theater marquees in the space of one block is almost too much for me to process. Ray instructs me to take my pick, and it is a hard decision. I would like to see the movie with the chariot race. The one that won the big Hollywood award. *Bender*, I think it is called and can't figure out why, since it is the term my mother uses to describe what my father is doing when he is drinking. Ray clears up my confusion when I ask him about it.

"No, not *Bender. Ben Hur,*" he explains with a loud belly laugh.

Ben Hur is not playing, so it comes down to a western with Rory Calhoun or a 3-D movie about giant insects. Ray favors the sci-fi flick, saying he is not much on movies that have more cattle than people. That is okay with me because I like scary movies, although I would like to see some western landscape in Technicolor.

We are handed our special 3-D cardboard glasses by a heavyset woman in the ticket booth and we enter the dark and musty theater, choosing a seat as close to the screen as our 3-D specs will allow. Too near to it and the effect is lost.

Before us a spaceship hurls toward earth to the accompaniment of eerie high-pitched music that sends chills up my back. Despite the horror on the screen, I am transported to a more wonderful place. All is right with the world in the cool, removed darkness. Movies are the refuge of my childhood, even ones about hideous aliens.

Over the River

IT IS SLIGHTLY AFTER 5 A.M. when I slip from the Scanlons' quiet apartment. My father has instructed me to meet him in his room at the crack of dawn. Ray has advanced him a few dollars but not enough for bus tickets. We will catch a ride with our thumbs, which should not be a problem, says my father.

He greets me with a loud, phlegmy hack when I enter his room. There he sits on the edge of his cot dressed and waiting. When he stoops to tie his shoe I notice an empty wine bottle behind his feet. My thoughts instantly return to the image of him lying stone-cold drunk outside my mother's basement apartment. When he notices that I have detected the bottle, he says that Leland dropped by last night and brought his own booze with him. He claims he has not touched a drop, but I suspect otherwise and am too anxious to get going to refute his story. This does not bode well for our long journey ahead, I think drearily.

Although it is fairly light outside, the streetlamps are still on, and there is almost no traffic because it is a weekend morning. My father suggests that we stop for a doughnut but there are no places open, so we head north to the George Washington Bridge. My father proclaims it the path to the Pacific in an attempt to brighten my spirits, which have been seriously dampened since discovering the wine bottle.

It takes us a good chunk of the morning to reach the bridge and about a half hour to walk across it. My father makes a few feeble attempts to hitch a ride but he says we need to get to the other end, where the conditions are more favorable for cars to stop. Someone could get killed if a car were to stop on the bridge, because there is no place to pull over, he observes. Then he launches into a lecture concerning the right and wrong way to hitchhike.

"People are dumb when it comes to thumbing a ride. They don't know where to stand, for one thing. It always makes me laugh when a hitcher stands on the entrance ramp to a highway. He loses all the traffic already up on the road heading in the direction he wants to go. Just as bad is some jerk who stands at the mouth of an exit when he's trying to get someplace down the highway. You got to use your noggin."

I ask him if he knows how highways are numbered and he says sure he does.

"How?" I ask, and he replies that it's a dumb question, since they're given all kinds of numbers.

"No, they're not," I say with professorial authority, and proceed to explain that roads west and east are given even numbers and that odd numbers are assigned to roads that go north and south.

"Well, smarty pants," he says after a long, calculated pause, "then how do they number highways that go northeast and southwest?"

I have no answer to what I protest is a trick question, and he gives me a look of mock triumph as we continue our march across the Hudson River.

By the time we get to the other side of the bridge my father looks pale and exhausted. I have seen him sick on many occasions, nearly always after a night of drinking. He leans against a railing and gags, but he doesn't vomit. Dry heaves, I have heard this called. I tell him that he should not have started drinking again and he says to shut my trap, that this has nothing to do with booze. He has some kind of bug, he says, claiming he probably got it from cleaning the crappy bathrooms at the Oxford Arms. Then he comments that he is not as young as I am and that this morning's hike has taken some wind from his sails. He searches his pockets for a match to light the cigarette that hangs from his mouth, and curses in frustration when he comes up empty-handed. This pleases and amuses me. Again his suffering seems an appropriate punishment for his breaking his promise to stay dry, and I hope the memory of this moment will be branded on his mind so that he will not fall off the wagon in the future, at least until we get out west. There, I figure, I can fend for myself if I have to. Maybe get a job at a ranch or movie studio. Fib about my age. I wonder how much older I will look when we get there.

After a few minutes he has recovered enough for us to continue and we walk another mile or so until he decides we are at the right place to try our luck. The sun is very intense and there is no shade in the vicinity. I attempt to escape the harsh rays by standing in my father's shadow, but he says we will have a better chance of snagging a ride if I stand where I can be seen by the passing cars.

"They know you're not going to rob them when you're with a kid," he says, all the while jingling the few coins in his pants pocket.

When I ask why he always shakes his change, he says it is a habit he picked up bellhopping.

"You always had pockets full of tips," he reflects. I say he does this because it makes him feel rich and important.

He does not appreciate my theory and tells me that it is a silly notion. He looks indignant and irritated and I wonder if I should carry the point further by adding that he really does it to impress people. This, I think, would probably be going too far, so I squelch the urge to turn the screw any further. This is the way I avenge the mess he has made of everyone's life, the method I use to even the score, so to speak. Sometimes I would like to tease him to tears.

The gusts created by the cars and trucks as they fly by hit us with a powerful force, and at times we are nearly blown off our feet. This only deepens my father's irritation with the world. After each heavy blast of polluted air he attempts to restore his hair's usual slicked-back look, but his efforts prove futile.

At one point the whole thing becomes too much for him and he tosses his plastic Ace comb at the passing traffic. I do the best I can to restrain myself from falling to the ground in a fit of laughter. The sight of him trying to regain control of his wildly flapping gray hair makes me nearly forget the hollowness in the pit of my stomach.

Purple People Eater

THE BLAZING SUN is overtaken by a fast-moving band of dark clouds. In the near distance there is the rumble of thunder. God is bowling, I think, recalling my mother's explanation for the phenomenon. My father says God's got gas. I like his explanation better. It has been at least two hours since we took up our position on the highway, and my father has the look of desperation in his eyes.

"These New Yorkers wouldn't pick up their own damn mother," he complains.

I know that were it not for his discovering a book of matches in our canvas grip we would not be here right now. During the last few minutes we have both relieved ourselves behind a clump of scrawny bushes that stands some thirty feet behind us. My stomach feels like it is about to snap, and I have never been so thirsty. There is no restaurant or store within sight, so to give in to our hunger and thirst would mean a temporary abandonment of our plan to get going and I am not about to let that happen.

On top of everything else, I have to move my bowels but am not inclined to do so behind the thin foliage. Peeing is one thing back there, but dropping my pants is out of the question. Now it is my father's turn to taunt me, and following my recent attacks on him he relishes the opportunity.

"'Fraid to do poop-poop,'" he teases, using a baby's voice. "Him going to poop in him little britches."

This gets to me and I shout for him to shut up, which he does after sticking out his tongue and making a goofy face. A half hour passes without either of us speaking or anyone offering us a ride.

It takes a lightning bolt hitting the ground a short distance from us to break our resolve, and we begin to dash for shelter. As we are jogging along the highway I casually extend my thumb and a car skids to a halt a few feet away. A figure inside a pink Hudson Hornet motions to us. Exchanging smiles with one another, we dash to the waiting car and climb aboard.

The driver is a guy I figure to be in his twenties. He is wearing a black T-shirt and has a pack of cigarettes rolled up into one of the sleeves, which strains to contain a bulging muscle. His hair is heavily greased and carefully combed into sleek fins like Scooter's was. The car radio is blasting "Flying Purple People Eater." When we are seated he floors the accelerator and we are hurled on our way like a human projectile from a circus cannon.

"Whar y'all headin'?" he asks in a thick southern drawl, but before we can answer he begins to sing along with the radio.

A photograph of an immensely obese young woman with a towering beehive hairdo is taped to the dashboard, upon which rests a quart bottle of Pabst Blue Ribbon beer. This sets off an alarm in me when I see my father eyeing it.

"Love this song!" bellows our driver as he improvises on the lyrics.

"'One thighed, one horny, flyin' purple peter eater ...' That's the color my willie is. My girl has this thing for purple, so I up and dyed it purple," he says, giving out a loud roar. "Okay, not really," he admits, "but I sure am thinkin' on it."

As he is chortling, his cigarette falls from his mouth into his lap. While he is frantically searching for it the Hudson veers into the next lane, missing an oncoming car by inches. My father is not amused and has a look that says he would rather be elsewhere.

Our driver finally retrieves the lit butt and gets the car back into the westbound lane.

"Shoot, almost toasted my purple peter. Hey, by the way, my handle's Jimmy Coe," he says. Without asking our names, he invites my father to partake of the beer that has somehow managed to stay in place on the dashboard.

To my great relief he refuses the offer. Our driver then removes the cap from the bottle and pretends to pour some into his lap.

"Jest in case there's still some sparks down there. Don't want to take any chances with the family jewels. It's my Sally May's favorite choker—get it?" he whoops, laughing so long and hard that I begin to lose control of myself as well.

My amusement is further heightened when I notice the needle on the speedometer passing the eighty mark. This is the fastest I have ever gone and I love the way the world flies by at this speed. The color that had momentarily returned to my father's face is absent again as we barrel through the Garden State's Watchung Mountains and onto the Piedmont, which leads to Pennsylvania. Our sudden rapid progress westward thrills me. I calculate that if we maintain our current velocity we will see prairie by late tomorrow, but then my hopes are dashed when our driver reveals that he is only going as far as Pittsburgh, where Sally May apparently lives. This seems to please my father, however, who clearly relishes the idea of getting out of the car as soon as possible.

He gets his wish temporarily when we stop for something to eat at a place called the Pocono Diner, nestled between two tall, wooded hills. Crudely carved into the wood frame of the screen door are the words POCO PUKE.

"Sounds good to me," says Jimmy Coe, who then states that his friends call him Acorn, which makes sense to me since he has two acorns tattooed on the inside of his left forearm.

I know what my father will say about his nickname when we are alone, but I have taken a liking to this guy, who seems to me to be fun incarnate. Not a damn care in the world, he tells my father as we descend the slope of an Appalachian peak in the dark at speeds that have us holding on for dear life.

Coming out of one of the more dramatic hairpin curves, he reveals that we are riding on bald tires, a fact that prompts my father to reach for the beer bottle. Fortunately it is empty by now.

"Jest kiddin'. Only the front ones got no tread," says Acorn, his thumb deeply embedded in his nostril. I have never witnessed anyone picking their nose with their thumb and am at once amused and disgusted, especially when he removes his thumb and wipes its large haul against his shirt.

Once the terrain has leveled somewhat the radio reception improves. As we pass a sign that says Pittsburgh is eighty-nine miles, Elvis and Acorn perform a duet.

"My Sally May goes nuts when I do Elvis the Pelvis. Specially when I shake like this," he tells us, his eyes off the road again for several seconds. To illustrate his point he rocks the steering wheel to and fro, causing the Hudson to weave and skid violently. "Makes her hot as a campfire. Can't keep her hands off me." He laughs and then places the tip of his cigarette against the photo of his beloved, burning a hole in the area of her crotch.

My father takes a butt from his pack and places it between his lips before realizing that he already has a lit one in his hand. His tension has returned in full force. Eventually I manage to doze off and when I wake up we are entering Pittsburgh, which I recall from my study of the Rand McNally is only a stone's throw from Ohio, the first state in the Midwest when you are coming from the East Coast. We have made a small but important dent in our journey and I am pleased.

Mission of Hope

THE PROBLEM OF WHERE we will spend the balance of the night is solved when Acorn announces that he does not want to bother his girlfriend at this late hour because she lives with her parents, so he plans to park his car near her house and snooze until it is daylight. He invites us to do likewise and we gladly accept.

In the morning Acorn's mood is subdued. He is no longer the wildly upbeat character of just a few hours before. As he is fishing through his crammed glove compartment for a pack of smokes to share with my father, the handle of a pistol appears and we catch sight of it. Aware of this, Acorn shoots us a menacing look and announces that he is going to blast Sally May when she walks out the front door of her parents' house. Following a prolonged, awkward silence, he bursts into laughter and comments that if we believe that one he has some nice property in the Everglades to sell us.

He locates his pack of cigarettes under the gun and divvies up its contents, insisting that my father take half. A few quick goodbyes and we part company, much to my father's obvious relief.

"They call that guy Acorn because he's nuts," comments my father as we leave the Hudson Hornet behind and head to the highway that will take us to Ohio and beyond.

"Do you think he was really going to shoot Sally May?" I ask as we shuffle along.

"Who knows," replies my father, and the conversation about Acorn is over.

The day is overcast and cool and by the time we reach the main artery west it is drizzling. We select a spot under a highway overpass and give hitchhiking a shot, but the conditions make it difficult for motorists to see us clearly. Catching a Greyhound is still not an option because we have less than three dollars to our name.

Given the circumstances, getting a lift today is unlikely, concludes my father after a long stretch of time has passed without the slightest nibble. He suggests we head downtown, where we might find a place to put our heads for the night. This rankles me, and I tell him he should go if he wants but I intend to stay put and catch a ride. The only thing I am going to catch is pneumonia, he says, and then assures me that no matter what the weather is tomorrow we will be on our way. My attempts to convince him to give it a further try are unsuccessful. We need a decent night's sleep, he comments, adding that the day is about shot anyway, even though it is only early afternoon.

Fortunately the rain lets up slightly as we walk toward town. Along the way we consult a telephone book and find a place listed called the Mission of Hope, which looks like it might offer us food and shelter. It is the best we can do under the circumstances, remarks my father, still hunting through the pages for an alternative.

It takes us almost two hours to reach the shelter, which is in a run-down neighborhood dotted with tiny bars. Men in worn and soiled clothes form a line that leads to the shelter's entrance, and we reluctantly join them. My father is clearly distressed by the scene. I am more than a little curious.

"We'll just check it out. Maybe they got a better place for people with kids," he says hopefully, and I think he is lucky to have me along if that is the case.

The man standing in front of us asks my father for a smoke and reports that the mission has the best beef stew in town. That brightens my spirits, but my father remains dubious as he hands over the cig.

"Thanks, Mac. Really appreciate it. Your boy?" he asks, pointing to me with a finger wrapped in bloodstained gauze.

His few remaining teeth are gray and rotted and even in worse condition than my father's. There are specks of dried blood on his chin, and one of his eyes protrudes as if it has been popped from its socket. A piece of twine holds his threadbare pants in place. What a terrible way to end up in life, I think, vowing that when I get older I will not turn out like these tattered figures standing in line.

My father inquires about the possibility of a family-type refuge in the area, but the old derelict does not know of any, at least none that take men. He says there might be a shelter that will take me though.

"They keep the kids and gals separate. Men are sent here. I got six kids, but they're all grown up. Ain't seen any of them in years. Got their own lives, so don't need the ole man. You know how it is," he says, savoring the last few drags of his borrowed smoke.

Eventually the line starts to move and soon we are inside the mission's stark lobby. A neatly groomed man in a white shirt sits behind a desk and requests that all who enter sign the ledger before him. He repeats these words to my father when it is his turn and adds, "God be with you," after we are signed in.

We pass through a set of doors that leads into a large room furnished with long tables and benches. The air is thick with the tantalizing aroma of food, but there is no sign of any. My stomach growls so loud that I imagine the noise echoing throughout the hall. Shiny metal pitchers filled with ice water have been arranged at carefully measured intervals on the tables.

The men who stood patiently outside in the dreary mist have selected where they will sit, and we do the same. Above our heads are two dangling strips of sticky flypaper. As we await the arrival of food, I attempt a body count of the most congested strip but soon give up in frustration because it twists and turns in the breeze, causing me to lose my place.

There are a couple of dead flies on our table near a water pitcher that look as if they have managed to escape a gooey fate only to perish within inches of a second chance. The scene reminds me of a cartoon depicting a man with a swollen tongue hanging from his mouth in a blistering desert succumbing an arm's length from a lush oasis. I slide closer to my father to get away from the direct drop zone of the densely occupied traps.

The men in the dining hall pay little attention to one another, and it is surprisingly quiet. Too quiet it seems to me until I realize that a religious service is about to take place. A tall figure in a black suit enters from a side door and climbs onto a small platform containing a lectern, and the man next to us comments that you have to work if you expect to get paid.

The austere-looking gentleman, who I assume is a minister, announces that he will be reading from Matthew, chapters 4 through 6. A rumble from my stomach punctuates his statement.

He begins with "Then was Jesus led up of the Spirit into the wilderness to be tempted of the Devil" and concludes a half hour later with "Sayeth the Lord. Amen."

The assemblage repeats his amen, and as if that is the magic word, several men in aprons enter the room carrying bowls, silverware, bread, and large pots of steaming beef stew. Before I get my first helping, I am thinking about seconds.

When a bowl is filled in front of me, I descend on it with savage fury, prompting my father to instruct me to take my time. Nonetheless I continue to gobble away with a vengeance. It tastes better than anything I can remember. An old bum across the table winks and nods at me as he wipes his wet mouth with a piece of white bread, something I have actually seen my father do. Meanwhile a man next to him appears to be close to gagging as he raises a spoon to his trembling lips.

I am suddenly having trouble getting a chunk of meat down my throat. No matter what I do it will not budge. I attempt to cough it up but my efforts fail to dislodge it. Something in me ignites and I am up on my feet waving my arms frantically. The large room begins to tilt, and sounds become muffled. It is like being under the surf at Coney Island, and I hope someone will rescue me again.

This time my father is my savior. He puts his fingers down my throat and extracts a chunk of unchewed beef from my windpipe. Air flows into my lungs, and the room rights itself. My father is shaken and curses the place for serving such tough chunks of horse-meat, as he calls it. Then he turns his wrath on me.

"Chew the goddamn stuff," he growls, and pushes his bowl away.

He has lost his appetite, but my close call has only slightly di-minished mine, and I return to my meal while my father eyes my every move. No one has apparently noticed the incident, or no one cares. The food has everyone's rapt attention.

Second helpings are not offered, but I have had my fill anyway. The men in the food hall gradually rise from the tables and disap-pear to another part of the shelter. We follow them and end up in an even larger room filled with beds. This is where we are to bunk for the night, we are told by the fellow with the protruding eyeball and wounded finger.

"Pick your sacks before they're a goner," he advises us.

We lay claim to two cots next to a far wall. It is too early to turn in but there is nothing else to do. Leaving our beds means running the risk of losing them, so we stay put like squatters on cherished turf. Within the hour the dormitory of vagrants is full. Latecomers are turned away. They might get sacks at the Sally, comments a bearded man on the bunk to the left of my father's.

"The Salvation Army," he explains while digging the remains of dinner from his teeth with a wooden matchstick. "It's just three blocks away. Been in that army myself a few times."

Except for a deep triangular scar on his forehead, I believe the man would make a perfect department-store Santa Claus, especially since his laugh is always in three distinct syllables, each beginning with a blasting *h* sound.

"If you're inclined to, you can get some pretty good money for your blood over at Med Lab up near Pitt. Eight bucks as of last week when I was there. Going back in a few days. Figure by then my veins will be filled up again. Not supposed to give blood too often.

Usually want you to wait a couple months between drawings, but I give it every couple of weeks. Easy money," says the man, who tells us to call him Riley.

"I'm not crazy about needles," admits my father, "but it's something to think about."

Later when I propose he do just that, he informs me that he wouldn't go within ten miles of any place in the business of draining people of their life-sustaining fluids, money or no money, and it is obvious from his solemn expression that this is a dead issue.

"Only babies are afraid of needles," I say tauntingly, and he reminds me that I cried when I had to get my polio shot.

While Riley and my father talk, I become increasingly amused by the antics of the same person who used his bread as a napkin. His bunk is across the aisle from mine, and while most of the street-weary men have collapsed like corpses on their bed, this one is engaged in a strange pantomime. Forming animal shapes with his hands, he conducts a battle between them while softly growling and barking. This continues for some time and in the end his left hand gets the better of his right hand.

The show is not over, however, because the man, who reminds me of Roy Rogers's sidekick, Gabby Hayes, removes a container from a crumpled bag next to his bed and begins to blow bubbles. I have never seen bubbles the size of the ones he makes and am doubly amused when one quivering globe descends on my father's head and remains there fully intact unbeknownst to him while he discusses the ins and outs of the hotel trade with Santa's derelict twin.

Bedbugged

THE LIGHTS ARE turned off promptly at 9:30 P.M. There are a few isolated pockets of conversation, but beyond that and occasional eruptions of coughing and spitting from different points in the dark, it is quiet. Sleep overtakes me quickly, and in my dream I am back in the drab living room of my mother's basement flat.

My sisters are playing tag and I join in by chasing Claudia down the hall toward the front door. Her arms are outstretched as she dashes forward in an attempt to elude my touch. There is a sudden crashing of glass, followed by a scream. Her arms are extended through the glass panes in the door and blood is shooting everywhere. My mother runs from the kitchen with a stack of towels to wrap around her wounds.

"You are supposed to watch out for your sisters, to protect them," she shouts at me while wrapping towel after towel around my injured sibling's shredded limbs. "You're just like your father. If you just did what was right, I would love you as much as I love your sisters!"

This is only one of many dreams this night in which my sisters become my unwitting victims. In another I am riding down a steep hill on the back of Pam's tricycle. She is pleading for me to slow down, but I continue undeterred, pushing at the ground with my foot to increase the speed. Partway down I leap off, leaving my baby sister on her own to continue the rapid descent. Before she reaches the bottom, the tricycle flips over and she is thrown face-first onto the pavement. Again my mother admonishes me for my neglectful behavior, and I promise with all my heart that I will do better and not be like my father.

In the middle of the night I am awakened by a stinging sensation near my knee and another on the back of my neck. When I probe the areas, I encounter something moving, a small bug. Filled with revulsion, I swiftly pitch my discovery into the surrounding blackness, but there is more movement around my feet and under my back.

My father is snoring when I leap from my cot and land on top of him. The first word from his mouth is my mother's name and then he sits bolt upright, sending me to the floor.

"Christ, what's the matter?" he asks, and I tell him about the living things crawling on me.

He removes his flashlight from our bag and shines it on my bed.

"Bedbugs," he says with complete disdain. "The goddamn hole is lousy with bedbugs."

We gather our belongings and begin to make our way out of the dormitory. When we are a few feet away from our cots, a hand grabs my arm and I let out a yell. My father pulls me toward him, freeing me from whatever unknown monster had me in its grip. This incident is immediately followed by barking and I recall the bubble man and his animal act. Someone nearby curses and says to shut up or he will break our necks and my father matches his threat with one of his own. The door we exit through deposits us into the mission's lobby.

When my father presses the handle of the main entrance door, he discovers that it is locked. We are trapped inside the Mission of Hope for the balance of the night. This is just as well, concedes my father, since there is no place to go during what he fittingly terms the dead of night.

"If we're walking the street at this hour, the cops will probably pick us up anyway."

There are two wooden benches, and I curl up on one of them. I fall asleep watching the tip of my father's cigarette alternate from a dull to a brilliant glow. It is as if I have entered my dreams midreel, because I am returned to the back of Pam's tricycle moments before it topples with her on it, leaving her face covered with thick purple scabs and ultimately scar tissue that will mark her for life in more ways than just physically.

"My pretty face!" she screams over and over as I lead her to our bunker abode. She receives first aid while I get another stinging rebuke from my hysterical mother.

"She's your baby sister. Are you trying to kill her? Don't you care?"

Far off I can hear my father's voice telling me not to cry and coaxing me from my troubled sleep.

Reborn

THE BREAKFAST SERMON is shorter than the one delivered at the previous night's meal. Before we partake of the oatmeal and coffee, neither of which appeals to me, the lanky mission preacher reminds his captive flock that the fruits of God sour in the mouths of sinners. After a collective amen that sounds more like a sigh of relief, the room is filled with the clank of spoons hitting the interior walls of countless ceramic bowls and cups.

Leaving our breakfast all but untouched—my father is no fan of oatmeal either—we head for the lobby. As we near our escape route we come head-to-head with the preacher. He asks if we have had enough to eat and we both answer in the affirmative. He can arrange for second helpings for me, he tells my father. A growing boy needs plenty of the Lord's sustenance, he says, and adds that he hopes my father has been teaching me the Bible. My father admits that he has been a little negligent in that particular area of my education but says he plans to enroll me in Sunday school when we reach California, where he will have a steady job and a chance to get my life back to normal.

" 'Now it is high time to awake out of sleep, for now is our salvation nearer than we believe,' " proclaims the preacher, gesturing dramatically with his right hand, which he then places on my shoulder.

"It is written that 'the night is far spent, the day at hand. Let us therefore cast off the works of darkness, and let us put on the armour of light.' "

Romans 12 is what he is quoting from, he informs us, and then asks my father if he may speak with me privately for a few minutes. My father hesitates, then reluctantly gives his consent. This is not all right with me and I make that clear to him by tightening my face and narrowing my eyes to tiny, angry slits. No matter, the preacher escorts me into a small office just off the lobby and closes the door. I am told to fear not, because God is in the room with us and wants to love me if I will let him.

We sit in chilly leather chairs facing one another.

"Let us pray for forgiveness," begins the preacher, who clamps his eyelids together and begins moving his lips in silence.

I watch him intently and am poised to close my eyes when I sense that he is about to open his. The whole thing strikes me as a sort of game or comedy sketch, and I am willing to play along if that will get us back on the road.

A minute or so passes in this manner, during which time I study a large, crusty mole above the minister's cheek. It reminds me of a larger version of the wart on my left thumb. Nothing has proved capable of removing it, except for an accident that temporarily left my digit wonderfully smooth. In a month the wart had grown back bigger and uglier than ever. Still I steadfastly refuse my father's offer to eliminate it once and for all with his Gillette razor.

"Are you a sinner, child?" asks the preacher, his eyes still tightly sealed.

I tell him that I don't think so, and he opens them and looks at me skeptically.

" 'If we say that we have no sin, we deceive ourselves, and the truth is not in us.' That is written in the Good Book," says the preacher in an admonishing tone. I am not sure I understand the meaning of this heavenly quote.

"The Bible also says, 'The wages of sin is death.' Do you want to burn in hell for an eternity? We are all sinners, son, and the first step to salvation is to admit this and open up your heart to Jesus."

I nod in agreement and wonder where this is going to lead. The preacher's expression grows more solemn as he moves his long face within inches of mine.

"Do you want to be spared the agony of damnation?"

Yes, I say, trying to add real conviction to my response.

"Of course you do, my son. Just hand your soul over to him, and you will reside in the Kingdom of Paradise forever. Admit that you are a sinner and repent. Become a true child of Christ and condemn Satan for his vile deeds against all mankind."

Seizing the opportunity to draw on the actor in me, I exhale loudly and rub at my eyes in an effort to convey the impression that I am deeply moved by the moment.

"Are you ready, my child, to offer your life to God? He will give you life everlasting. Are you open to the Lord?" inquires the preacher, his hands raised skyward and the vessels in his temples bulging from his face.

"Yes," I say, expecting blood to come gushing out of his ears. "Sure."

"Praise God Almighty!" cries the preacher, dropping his hands to my shoulders. "Hallelujah! You are saved and reborn unto Christ. Let us pray."

This time I shut my eyes along with the preacher and keep them closed until he breaks the silence by asking me if I feel the presence of the Lord in my heart. I tell him that I think so, and he can hardly contain his joy.

"You are now God's servant," he informs me, squeezing my arms tightly.

On our way out of his office, he presses something into my hand. I know by the feel of it that it is money. When we reenter the lobby my father is standing near the entranceway drawing on a cigarette.

"You've got a real good boy here, mister," remarks the preacher.

"Yeah, especially when he's sleeping," cracks my father.

The preacher misses the humor in his comment and tells him that I have just embraced the Lord and am reborn as a God-fearing Christian.

"Would you care to do the same?" asks the preacher, apparently eager for another conversion.

My father declines the offer, saying that we need to get going in order to catch a ride that has been promised us by a friend, an old hotel racket buddy of his. The preacher admonishes him for taking salvation so lightly, and my father pledges to take action in that department as soon as he can.

"Tomorrow may be too late, sir. Make your peace with the Lord now and you too shall be saved from a certain fiery fate. There's no opportunity for salvation on the other side of the grave."

"I know," says my father, who then leads me through the door to the street.

The day is bright and mild. A perfect day for hitching a ride, I happily surmise. When we are out of sight of the mission, I show my father the five-dollar bill I have been rewarded for being reborn. "Good going," he says, patting me on the back, and I feel like I have just hit a home run out of Yankee Stadium.

Within minutes of reaching the route that leads westward, we hook a ride clear to Indiana and I think that maybe someone upstairs is indeed now watching over us, or at least me.

PART II
PITTSBURGH TO INDIANAPOLIS
(366 Miles)

Pearl's Place

IT IS DUSK when we arrive in Indianapolis and find our way to the bus terminal where my father seeks out a Travelers Aid station, whose purpose, he says, is to help travelers in need, and there is no doubt that we are in need. In quick order we are dispatched to a boardinghouse about a mile away by a Travelers Aid worker. She explains that the woman who runs the place is one of the nicest people in the world.

"I'm sure she'll let you stay there until you get your check in the mail," remarks the aid, who looks to be about the age of my mother but is much heavier and not as pretty.

My father has told her that a check from his former employer back in Albany—the DeWitt Clinton Hotel, he adds for the sake of authenticity   is being mailed to him by my mother, who eventually plans to follow us to California when my sisters finish out their school year. The woman does not ask for an explanation as to why I am not completing the school year and my father does not volunteer one.

The streetlight outside the boardinghouse is not working and there are two huge trees in front of the structure that block almost everything from view except for a portion of porch. A figure from the shadows greets us as we stand beyond a picket fence that appears about to burst onto the sidewalk from the weight of a million wildflowers and shrubs pressed against it.

"Come on in. You must be the folks that Millie down at the Greyhound called about," says a woman who introduces herself as Pearl.

She owns the place, she tells us proudly as we are escorted inside and given a tour of the house. She and her dead husband bought the old Victorian back in 1934, she reports, and points out the narrow strips of stained glass that frame the front door.

"Wallace, that was my husband's name, was a glassmaker and he put that in. He was a very talented man, but he got terrible arthritis in his hands, so he had to stop doing it. There's more upstairs, but I don't think it's as pretty as these."

During her narrative my father manages to interject his "check is in the mail" story. This is not a problem to Pearl, who says that we should just make ourselves at home and that things have a habit of righting themselves.

There is something about her that is extremely appealing to me. It is not her appearance, whose only distinct feature is a long gray braid accented with a red ribbon, but rather her kindly manner. She is the epitome of the sweet aunt persona, a virtual manifestation of goodness and caring.

"The other boarders are usually in the living room around this time, but since the TV is in the repair shop everyone pretty much finds someplace else to be," she comments as we are led up a flight of stairs to our room.

Auntie Pearl, as I am already calling her in my mind, informs us that the sheets are changed on Saturdays and that visitors must leave the premises by ten o'clock. Halfway down the corridor we pass a room whose door is open. Inside is a strikingly attractive teenage girl who is sitting on the edge of the bed painting her toenails the same bright color as the ribbon adorning Pearl's hair. She is wearing a long pink T-shirt that barely covers her smooth thighs. My father turns away when the girl looks in our direction.

"That's little May. She's in room five. She's going to be a famous model. Taking a course down at the Hoosier Palace of Cosmetology right now so that she knows how to use makeup for the close-ups," reports Pearl, more for the girl's benefit than ours, I suspect.

The young woman smiles and says hello as we pass, and I feel the blood stream into my cheeks.

"You're in six. Actually, only I know that, because as you can see there's no numbers on the doors," says Pearl, trying to find the key to the room in the sagging pocket of her ankle-length skirt.

A few more attempts at unlocking the door with the wrong key and we gain entrance. The room is spacious and features a sink with running water, two large, curtained windows, and an overstuffed wing chair covered with blue seagulls, among other homey objects. Pearl points out that the bathroom is down the hall on the left, information that is not so crucial to us since we have a sink to pee in and I haven't done number two since we left New York anyway. Breakfast is served at seven on weekdays and at eight-thirty on weekends, she says, then departs, leaving us to bask in the luxury of our newest interim accommodations.

The day's trip has done me in and I slide under the knobby bedspread, which smells deliciously clean and fragrant. The last thing my conscious mind records is my father picking at his tired and bloodshot eyes in a mirror above the sink. As I drift off I hear my mother calling for me and my sisters as we play hopscotch on the sidewalk in front of Joe Oliver's barbershop, situated directly across the street from our apartment. There is an edge to her voice as if something is not right. It is pretty much the tone the world knows her by.

The Little Family

OUR PASSAGE WEST is to be delayed again while my father attempts to raise enough cash to buy us a ticket to Denver. He says that if we can get that far in one jump, it will be a breeze catching a ride the rest of the way. I am annoyed by his scheme and demonstrate my displeasure by tossing my dusty canvas shoe across the room. Luckily it misses a large ceramic vase containing a bouquet of plastic flowers.

I will get us thrown out if I don't behave, contends my father, and I say that is okay with me because then we would have to get going. He tosses my shoe back to me, and I put it on over socks that have already developed holes in the toes and heels, which have hardened from dirt and sweat. Somewhere along the line my other pair has been lost, and my father speculates it may have fallen out of our grip back in Pittsburgh during our retreat from the bug-infested mattresses. He mentions nothing about plans to replace the socks, and it is not a real concern to me either.

Pearl introduces us to her other boarders when we appear in the dining room for breakfast. It is with some reluctance that we show up because neither one of us is thrilled about entering a room filled with total strangers.

"Everybody, I'd like you to meet the newest members of our little family. This is Mr. Keith and his youngster, Mitchell."

My father nods tentatively to the group and says to call him Curt and that my name is actually Michael. Pearl apologizes for the mistake and continues her introductions.

Seated clockwise around the table are Mr. Mosely, who says to call him Ole Moses and grumbles when Pearl refers to him as a retiree; a truck driver named Ben from North Dakota, sporting a meticulously sculpted handlebar mustache and the type of undershirt that musclemen wear; Vera and her son, Dennis, who Ben says is really called Squirt because he piddles his pants all the time; and May from last night.

Pearl comments that there is a member of the household named Waller, who regrettably is unable to join the group because of ill health. Ben adds that Mr Walrus, as he calls him, is too fat to move, so he takes all of his meals and anything else he can swallow in bed. Pearl scolds him for being rude and insensitive and he snickers, grabs a piece of toast, and leaves the table, announcing that he has to get a load of wire to Terre Haute by noon. Pearl calls after him to take some sausage for the road but the only reply she receives is the slamming of the screen door that leads to the front porch.

I am directed to a chair next to May and I am nearly overcome by the sweet scent of her perfume, which reminds me a little of the pink bubblegum that comes with baseball cards. From the corner of my eye I notice that she has shorts under the shirt she was wearing when we first laid eyes on her, and this disappoints me.

After breakfast my father embarks on his own to a place called Manpower, not far from the bus station. Pearl has told him it specializes in short-term employment for the able bodied. He will be back soon if there is no work for him and later if there is, he says, and leaves me sitting on the porch steps with stern instructions to stay put.

"Don't wander off," he warns, relighting the stub of a previously smoked cigarette. "You don't know this area, so hang out in the room. Maybe the landlady can find you some magazines to look at."

Despite my father's orders I pass part of the morning surveying the neighborhood while contemplating the significance of our having made it as far as the Midwest and the very state where Cary Grant was menaced by a crop-dusting plane that chased him across a cornfield in the movie *North by Northwest.* When I check our location on the map, I calculate that if we were the same distance inland from the West Coast we would be somewhere in Utah and still very much in the West. So we have not really gotten that far, I grimly surmise, and that realization dampens my mood significantly. I wonder why they call Indiana the Midwest and not the East.

The little boy nicknamed Squirt greets me on the porch of the boardinghouse when I return. He is every bit as skinny as me, maybe skinnier. His eyes are red and puffy and there are tracks on his cheeks where tears have cut a path through a layer of dirt. When I ask him why he is crying, he says that his mom got mad at him because he wet his pants again. There are fresh bruises above his right elbow, and when I inquire about them he says he fell down. He tries to conceal the pee stain on his khaki shorts, but his hands are not big enough to cover the entire dark circle.

"Ole Moses talks to the stars, you know," he says, squatting down in front of me.

Both of his front teeth are missing, and when he talks his tongue pokes through the gap, pushing tiny beads of saliva over his lips.

"Out back, on the rock, he cuts things with a knife. My mom says his marbles are lost somewhere."

May appears from inside the house, dressed in a tight-fitting skirt and blouse and high heels that make her wobble slightly as she walks. She offers us each a stick of Beech-Nut gum and tells us that she is waiting for her man friend. The odor of her perfume is stronger than it was at the dining room table, and her lips appear much larger because they are plastered with ruby-red lipstick. She tells us her gold-filled earrings are a present from the man who is about to pick her up.

"He's real nice. Buys me pretty things all the time. Lots of my man friends give me presents. They're real good to me."

I am transfixed by the deep dimples in her peach-colored cheeks and by her pale blue eyes. She looks to me like a cross between Sandra Dee and Doris Day, and I have never felt so attracted to a girl before.

She offers us another piece of gum, but out of politeness I decline. Squirt accepts her generous offer with considerable enthusiasm as a car pulls up, and within seconds she is carried away on her date. Squirt confides that he likes May because she never teases him about peeing his pants. A short time later, when Pearl calls us inside for a snack, referring to me as Mitchell once again, I notice that the dark spot on Squirt's pants has gotten bigger.

Big Boy

THE DOOR TO Mr. Waller's room is ajar and for some reason he knows that I am passing. He calls me by the name Pearl confuses for mine and asks me to come in. A soiled sheet covers most of his mountainous torso, which rests atop an acutely sagging mattress. A mound of pillows has been erected behind his perspiring bald head and shoulders to give him enough elevation to see the Muntz portable television set that is strategically positioned on a table at the foot of his bed. He reminds me of a picture of Khrushchev that I saw on the cover of a magazine, but he is even fatter. Waller and the Head Red, as my father calls him, share another unpleasing characteristic. They both have a knobby boil on their face that looks like the start of another head to me.

"New here, huh? Pearl told me about you and your dad. I can tell people by their footsteps, you know. Your old man's are odd, like he walks on the side of his feet or on an angle. Bet the soles of his shoes are worn thin on their outsides. Yours are light and energetic. Gazellelike. Different from Squirt's though, more spaced. That's because you're taller and older. You can learn a lot about folks from the way they walk. For instance, you can't really hear the footsteps of a strangler. Kind of like a tiger or lion stalking something to kill. Stealthy . . . floating like. So you don't hear them. Guess there are footsteps even when there's no apparent sound. Ever think about that, Mitchell?"

I admit to him that I have not, and he asks me how I like the place but does not stop talking long enough to let me reply, and I wonder why adults ask questions that they really do not want answered.

His voice is guttural and juicy, the kind I associate with chubby people, and it puts me in mind of sausages and pork chops and other greasy things that gurgle and snap in big iron skillets. He wants me to run an errand for him. I am told to go to the Big Boy restaurant a few blocks away and bring him back a super cheeseburger deluxe with extra onions and pickles and two extra slices of cheese. With his thick, stubby fingers he digs for several coins in a small black change purse propped on his bare chest. Just enough, he says, finally dislodging his fingers and handing me the necessary amount. Hurry, he orders, and I wonder what is in it for me, hoping that I will be rewarded when I return.

On my trip back to the boardinghouse, I am tantalized by the enticing aroma coming from the bag containing the burger. At one point I open it and inhale deeply. Will Mr. Waller notice that a small piece is missing? I wonder, but decide against nibbling at the tasty morsel, figuring that he may tip me enough to buy my own super cheeseburger deluxe or at least a regular-size burger.

Mr. Waller is delighted to see me and grabs the bag out of my hands as I approach the side of his bed. With lightning speed he unwraps the contents and begins gorging himself. Between gulps he instructs me to close the door to his room on my way out. I am disappointed and perturbed by his lack of generosity, but more than that I am in pain for my own Big Boy. If he asks me to get him another super cheeseburger deluxe, I resolve to take a massive bite from it. Better still, I plan to eat the whole thing and tell him I accidentally lost the money he gave me to buy it—it slipped from my hand into a sewer, or something plausible like that. In any event I plot to avenge his stinginess and treat my longing taste buds to what now seems to me the most delicious edible in the universe.

On my way out of Mr. Waller's room he lets out the loudest burp

I have ever heard, followed by a long succession of equally roaring farts. I speculate that it will probably not be too long before I am asked to make another trip to the Big Boy restaurant, because whenever I burp, my appetite returns larger than it was before the gassy eruption.

Liquids and Last Suppers

MY FATHER RETURNS to Pearl's in midafternoon looking haggard and spent. He says that he has worked the morning addressing envelopes for a racing magazine and that he can get in a few more hours doing the same thing tomorrow. There is something about his manner that makes me suspect he has been drinking. I move as close to him as possible to see if I can detect the scent of liquor on his breath, but he knows what I am up to and backs away.

"What's the matter with you?" he asks defensively, and I give him a look that says his secret is out of the bag. "You worry too much. You're like your old lady. Always smelling smoke where there's no fire," he counters, keeping his distance from me.

I scan his trouser pockets for the telltale bulge of a bottle, but there is none. To divert my attention he extends the top plate of his false teeth from his mouth, which at least covers his three remaining and decaying bottom teeth. He then crosses his eyes and tilts his head from side to side. He has done this a dozen times to get a rise out of me, but I am not buying it this time.

"You're a damn sourpuss," he says, sucking his uppers back into his mouth and flopping onto the bed.

While he dozes I gaze out the window at the field behind the boarding house and see Squirt playing alone in the middle of the tall grass. Loneliness comes barreling in on me, and an intense longing for my sisters brings a lump to my throat. When I try to swallow, tears fill my eyes and the view outside the window becomes a prism of distorted trees and clouds. I miss Claudia and Pamela but not enough to give up my dream of going out west. How grand it would be if we could all be taking the trip together as do families who are more fortunate.

After we have a supper of meat loaf, roasted potatoes, and iced tea, Ben regales Squirt and me with accounts of his life as a truck driver while we sit on the front porch. Until now I have not noticed that his left eye is two different colors. Three-quarters of it is blue, with the balance consisting of a triangular wedge of brown. This intrigues me and I study it for as long as I can without being caught.

With great dramatic effect he recalls the time his brakes gave out as he was driving down a steep slope in the Great Smoky Mountains, but just as he is about to reach the story's exciting finale, he falls silent. We are upset by this and demand that he tell us what happened. Following another carefully timed pause, he says that he was killed. Before we have a chance to digest this statement, he laughs, and we realize that we have been duped.

Next he tells me that he can remove a hair from my head without my feeling it. That is impossible, I respond, and he asks if I would like to make a little wager. He removes a dollar bill from the pocket of his dungarees and says it is mine if I feel the hair being plucked from my scalp. Although I cannot match his dollar with one of my own, I agree, believing this to be a sure thing.

Squirt is all eyes as Ben selects a strand of hair to remove from my head. On the count of three he says that he will perform this painless surgery, and I brace myself for the yanking sensation that is certain to follow.

Ben begins the count, and a split second later I feel a hand come down hard on the top of my head. This catches me completely by surprise and I do not know how to react. The pain from the blow dissipates faster than my humiliation and anger.

"Bet you didn't feel this come out of your bean, did you?"

asks Ben, proudly exhibiting the single strand of brown hair he has extracted.

I protest that he did not play fair, and he counters by stating that he did exactly what he said he would, that is, remove a hair without my feeling the hair being removed.

"Did you feel this being pulled out, young'n?" he inquires, the eyebrow above his multicolored eyeball arching quizzically.

"Well, not exactly," I admit. "But I sure felt you whack me," I add, letting the matter drop, figuring that if I persist he will want to collect the dollar he won.

Squirt requests that a hair be taken from his head too and Ben is more than willing to oblige. Tears well up in Squirt's eyes after being slapped, but in the same instant he begins to giggle and rub his head. It is obvious that he is no stranger to this kind of treatment.

We ask Ben to tell us another trucking story and he recounts the time he picked up a hitchhiker who turned out to be a vampire just like the ones in those Vincent Price movies. Squirt clutches his genitals as Ben describes in graphic detail how he had to drive a spike through the bloodsucker's heart.

As if on cue, there is a bloodcurdling scream from inside the house. Pearl is yelling for help. Ben leaps to his feet and we follow him through the screen door and into the house.

"It's Mr. Waller," shouts Pearl from the far end of the hall. "I think something's the matter," she cries, waving Ben on.

We are close behind as he dashes to the scene but we stop just inside the door to Mr. Waller's room as Ben approaches the still form on the bed. An arm is hanging limply to within inches of the floor, its chubby hand clutching the wrapper of a Big Boy burger. Pearl backs up to where we are huddled and gives out a faint whimper as she pulls us to her sides.

"Dead as they get," pronounces Ben, looking under Mr. Waller's drooping eyelids.

Squirt frees himself from Pearl and runs from the scene, clutching his pants.

"Looks like the poor bastard ate his last meal. Bet he drowned from the weight of his own body fat. Heard that can happen when you're as big as he was," adds Ben, moving the sheet over Mr. Waller's rigid face.

A half hour later two ambulance attendants strain to get the body through the front door. When they inquire about a more spacious exit, Pearl informs them that all the doors in the house are the same size and then warns them not to damage her late husband's stained glass. This inspires unhappy mumblings from the frustrated medics.

By exerting extraordinary effort they manage to shift the corpse sideways enough to squeeze it out onto the porch. Ben says he would gladly lend a hand were it not for his hernia, and my father, who has finally returned from a trip to the store for a pack of cigarettes, hangs in the shadows, unwilling to get involved in the fiasco.

The attendants succeed in getting the body partway down the porch steps before one of them loses his grip on the stretcher, sending Mr. Waller plunging to the ground. They stand there looking like Laurel and Hardy as Pearl collapses into her rocking chair.

"Well, you got him down the stairs, fellas. The rest shouldn't be that hard. Maybe you can just roll him the rest of the way," says Ben sarcastically, while Pearl fans her flushed face with the hem of her apron.

The whole gruesome spectacle has taken a toll on my stomach and I cannot get the smell of the Big Boy super cheeseburger deluxe out of my nostrils. The thought crosses my mind that it may have been the very burger that I delivered to Mr. Waller that killed him. Will I be a suspect in his death? I wonder. Later I will overhear Pearl telling a policeman that Mr. Waller ate every bit of the meat loaf dinner she had given him that evening, and I will feel somewhat exonerated.

"They got Mr. Walrus in the meat wagon," reports Ben, who is sternly scolded by Pearl for his callous disregard for the recently departed, as she puts it.

"How would you like to spend the last years of your life unable to get out of bed?" she adds.

"If I could get the kind of service he did, I'd say fine," responds Ben at a volume only we can hear.

My father escorts me to our room on the second floor and positions me at the sink in case my nausea gets the better of me, but by now the quaking in my abdomen has subsided and I can actually detect the return of my appetite.

Good Morning, Breakfast Clubbers

THE SMELL OF BACON sends me rushing downstairs the next morning. Domenico Modugno is singing "Volare" on the record player in May's room and there is a black-and-blue mark on Squirt's neck. Pearl says good morning as she enters the dining room carrying a plate of steaming grub.

"Eat up, everyone. The living must go on living," she says, attempting to dispel the gloom created by Mr. Waller's untimely passing.

Her eyes reveal a lack of sleep and this is the first time I have seen her without a braid. The way her gray hair hangs down on the side of her face makes her look older and a little like a witch. The only thing my father wants is coffee and a smoke. Not much of an appetite in the morning, he tells Pearl, who insists he take some bacon wrapped in a piece of toast for later.

"You can't work on an empty stomach, Mr. Keith," she says, and he heads off, sandwich in hand, to his job addressing envelopes.

With nothing better to do, I join Ole Moses in the living room while he listens to a radio program. Although it is summer he is wearing a knit hat and heavy wool pants held in place by suspenders. In contrast to this, his upper body is clad in a light cotton short-sleeved jersey with green and orange stripes. It is far too small and his substantial belly protrudes beneath it.

"Don McNeill's *Breakfast Club*," he tells me as I enter. "My favorite program. Comes from Chicago. Been listening to it for years. Better than the stuff on the picture set. You like it too, huh?"

"It's a real good show," I say, adding that I'm going to be on the radio someday too. I keep my eyes focused on his weathered hands as he pries dirt from under his thick fingernails with a pocketknife.

"It's Swiss Army," he says, taking note of my gaze. "A real beauty. Just bought it last week. Lost my other one and can't for the life of me figure out where. Give you two bits if you come across it in your travels, young man. Got a red handle on it like this one."

He shushes me as I am about to respond because he wants to sing along with the voices coming from the radio.

" 'Good morning, breakfast clubbers. How are you? ...' "

He is up on his feet and dancing around the living room when Pearl enters and tells him to calm down or he might be the next to drop dead. Her admonition has little effect. Instead, he grabs her by the hand and forces her to join in his merriment.

"Only live once, Pearl, honey, so you got to do what pleases you when the urge sets in."

This tickles more than angers her and they spin around the room in happy abandon.

Later, when I go to my room to get my yo-yo, I encounter May walking from the bathroom in a two-piece leopard-skin bathing suit, which I momentarily mistake for her underwear. She greets me with a warm smile and invites me into her room for some chocolate-covered cherries.

As she walks ahead of me I focus on her slender rump, which sways like a hula dancer's. I have never been in the presence of a girl like this and I am simultaneously excited and intimidated. The whites of her buttocks peek out from under her swimsuit and create a pleasing contrast with the tan of her upper thighs. Something unfamiliar and curious stirs in me and craves the sight of the balance of this mysterious and untanned region.

In her room she asks if she has shown me her pretty clothes, and I shake my head no. There is nothing solemn about her mood despite the sad events of the previous night. With substantial pride she opens the door to her crammed closet and begins describing each bright garment and who gave it to her. It seems that everything she owns is a present from some male caller, as she puts it.

"This is my favorite," she declares, taking a pale blue cashmere sweater from a crowded shelf. "Just got this from Billy . . . Mr. Hart, that is. He's an automobile sales executive and very rich," she adds, pronouncing *automobile* as if each syllable were a grand word in its own right. "He's so nice. Might come by tomorrow, if he can get free. Would you like to meet him?"

I say sure but do not really mean it, and run my hand over the sweater at her prompting. What she is most proud of is her earring collection, stored in a large vinyl jewelry box. When the top is opened it plays a tune I cannot identify. She tells me that it is called "I Can See an Angel" and that it is one of her all-time favorite songs.

"Patsy Cline sings it. Got the record if you want me to play it. You ever hear of her? She's the best girl singer in the world. Her daddy was a blacksmith, you know. I read all up on her, 'cause I love her so much."

A while into the tour, she remembers that she has invited me to her room for some chocolate-covered cherries. However, after an extensive search she declares that she must have eaten the last one without realizing it and she apologizes. I pretend that it is no big deal, and she offers me a flattened caramel that she discovers in the depths of her purse.

She wants to know what my mother is like and why I am not with her. Kids should always be with their mama, she declares. I use my father's story to explain the situation and she is happy that we will be reunited in California. Her mother is dead, she explains. Killed by a truck at twenty-two years old. She was only four when it happened, and since then she has lived with foster parents who never cared a whole lot for her.

"My foster daddy used to hit me and do things to me sometimes."

I am curious about what those things were, but she does not elaborate. Instead she says I will have to leave because she has to get ready for a date. On the way out of her room she says maybe we can become real good friends, and then a thought occurs to her and she tells me to wait a second. She has a summer shirt that she says is more for a boy than for a girl and she wants me to have it.

"I really won't wear it, and you look like you could use something different on," she comments, digging through a box next to her closet door. "Your daddy ought to get you some new britches too. Those look like they come over on the Pronto."

Responding to my obvious confusion regarding this reference, she elaborates.

"The *Nina, Pronto,* and *Santa Marino,*" she says, and I correct her.

"Yeah, them," she agrees, as if she had the names right to begin with. "Those boats with all them Pilgrims."

When she locates the shirt and hands it to me, I am pleased. It is dark green and does look more like a boy's than a girl's, but then I notice a small red flower embroidered at the bottom. May sees my disappointment and says that if I tuck it into my pants it will be hidden, but the idea of wearing it is now out of the question.

"I think I got some britches you could wear too. They have a button-up fly, but so what. I'll look for them later. Probably too big for you though. You're a pretty scrawny fella, ain't you? Well, you better get going so I can pretty up. Change that shirt, okay?"

A short while later I watch from the hall window as she is picked up by a guy in a shiny white Pontiac convertible. Although I attempt to conceal myself behind the curtain, May catches sight of me and waves. I pretend that I am not there until the car pulls away.

Wheeler-Dealers

BEN HAS INVENTED a car cleaner and wax he calls Modern Mobile Magic and he offers me a chance to get rich with him. For every container of the pasty substance I sell, he will reward me with stock in the product as well as a half-dollar.

"You can really make some serious buckaroos with this stuff. It works better than any car cleaner out on the market. You can't buy this in stores either. Maybe someday, but not right now," he boasts, leading me down the stairway to the basement of Pearl's house, where he has set up shop.

"Been working on this secret formula for a long time and now it's perfected. Once I get things rolling I'm going to quit the trucking business and give it all my time. You'll be the first one in on this and maybe even a partner someday if you sell a bunch. Be the youngest zillionaire in the country."

My heart races with the prospect of having so much money that I can take a train wherever I want to go and eat all my meals in the dining car like the really rich people do. In the far corner of the basement there is a long workbench with two large gas burners on top of it surrounded by several tall metal pots and cartons and bottles of the material he apparently uses to concoct his miracle potion. The foremost ingredients appear to be Tide laundry detergent and Ajax cleanser because I count at least thirty containers of the stuff strewed about the area. A half dozen cardboard boxes are neatly stacked a few feet from the workbench, and it is from one of these that Ben removes a container of his invention.

"Here it is. Like the artwork? I designed it myself," says Ben, holding it ceremoniously in his outstretched hand.

I am impressed with the label, which consists of a cartoon of a car with a broadly smiling bumper speeding across a road formed by the name of the cleaner.

"This stuff is going to make me a rich man, and you too, little partner. All you got to do is take it to some gas stations and car washes around here and tell them that it is the best way to return the natural luster and beauty of a car's paint job. Tell them nothing works better. That it's truly amazing what a little bit of Modern Mobile Magic will do for a car's finish. Just rub it on and wipe it off ten minutes later, and your car is as pretty as the day it was bought. Maybe prettier. Think you can do that, Mikey?"

"Sure," I say, and Ben sticks out his hand for me to shake.

"Then we got ourselves a deal. Take a can along with you to show, and write down their orders in this little book, okay? Tell them for every five cans they order, they get another one at half price."

"Okay," I say, hardly able to wait until he gives me the go-ahead to begin spreading the gospel of the world's greatest car cleaner.

After a few more minutes of instruction and pep talk from Ben, I head out to a garage I have seen a few blocks away. By the time I get there, my enthusiasm has turned to apprehension. The grown-up I see standing inside Rusty's Texaco makes me question my abil ity to convince anybody, especially an adult, of the virtues of Modern Mobile Magic. Despite my fears and doubts, I take a deep breath and enter the garage office.

"Can I help you, sonny?" asks the grease-covered man in a Texaco Fire Chief cap, seated on top of a pile of new Firestone tires.

"Yes, sir," I say, working hard to keep my voice from trembling and my legs from shaking. "I am here to ask you to stock the best car cleaner and shiner in the world ... Modern Mobile Magic."

"Modern what?" asks the man, leaning forward to get a closer look at the container I am holding up.

"Modern Mobile Magic. It makes cars look like new again. All you do is rub it on and wipe it off and the luster is returned so that it is prettier than ever."

"How much is it, boy?"

"A dollar thirty-nine to you, and you can sell it for two dollars. If you order five containers, the next one is half off."

"How do I know it does what you say it does, sonny?"

"It's really good because many people have used it," I reply, not prepared to have the merits of Ben's wonder product challenged.

"Yeah, but how do I know if it really works?"

"My father uses it all the time on his car, and it's shinier than any car in the neighborhood," I respond, figuring that it's fair play to tell a little fib in this particular situation, and besides, I can think of little else to offer in defense of Modern Mobile Magic.

"Tell you what," says the garage operator, "my car is out back. Why don't you prove that it works like you claim by cleaning it with that stuff? If it does such a good job, I'll order a few cans. What do you say?"

My instincts tell me this is not such a good offer but I accept, hoping it will lead to an order and dollars in my pocket.

"You won't be sorry," I say, and am ushered outside to his waiting car, a dark green Buick Roadster.

"Here's the hose so you can give it a good washing down before you put that stuff on. I got work to do. Come in and get me when you're done. Better be good if you expect me to sell that to my customers."

The car on which I am to demonstrate the stunning performance of Modern Mobile Magic isn't all that dirty and a quick hosing reveals a pretty fair shine to begin with. With the rags I have been provided I apply generous amounts of the cleaner to the car and in no time have it thoroughly covered. After waiting the prescribed amount of time to allow the solution to do its work, I attempt to wipe off what has become an immovable powdery gray blanket. No amount of desperate effort pierces the armorlike coating and I begin to panic.

"Oh, God help me!" I plead to myself as I try in vain to get Ben's secret formula off at least one small section of the car, but no deal— God is not listening.

"How's it coming, boy?" asks the garage man, sticking his head out of the office, and I assure him that he'll soon have the best-looking car in town.

There is no getting the cleaner off the car, I grimly surmise after another quarter hour of intense effort, so I decide to slip away before the garage guy comes to check on my progress. Within minutes I am back at Pearl's and looking for Ben, who happens to be at work in his basement laboratory.

"How'd it go, partner?" he asks, and I tell him the whole grisly story.

"Maybe I got the percentages mixed up. Just keep away from that garage. I don't want to have to pay for a paint job. I'll throw that batch out and restock so you can go out again. Sorry, buddy, these things happen sometimes. Could be too much Ajax. I'll double-check the measurements and we'll be back up and running in no time."

Not with me, I vow to myself. Back in my room I discover that Modern Mobile Magic is nearly as impossible to remove from my hands as it is from the surface of a Buick Roadster.

Vera's Prescription

THERE IS A SOFT TAPPING on my door, and Squirt is standing on the other side when I open it. His mother wants to see me, he says, without giving a reason why.

Their room is cluttered and messy. Its double bed is unmade and its sheets and blankets are piled in a heap on the floor next to another mound consisting of clothing. Mrs. Lange, or Vera, is wearing a wrinkled housedress that is unbuttoned down the front. The bones of her chest are perceptible through skin that is covered with red blotches. She greets me while attempting to brush a large knot out of her thin brown hair. When she gives the knot a hard tug, a bald spot is evident. She says something about how hard it used to be to get gum out of her hair when she was little and tosses the brush across the room in heated frustration. It bounces off the wall and strikes Squirt on the leg, but he does not flinch and stands perfectly still as if riveted to the floor.

Vera casts an unsympathetic look his way and removes a small piece of paper from a dresser drawer and presents it to me. "Would you do me a favor, Michael, and get this for me at the drugstore? Not the one across from the park, but the one on Hyde Street. It's just a few blocks farther. Go to the corner and take a left. Go straight until you come to it. I'd have Dennis do it, but he's too young to send that far."

She instructs me to tell the druggist that I am getting the pre-scription filled for my mother. If he asks I am to tell him that my mom has a very bad infection and diarrhea, but I am not to give him the boardinghouse address, she says. To dispel my apparent cu-riosity, she hands me a five-dollar bill and tells me to get sundaes with the change. "They got real good butterscotch sundaes at the fountain in that place. Now get going, and bring the ice cream back with you. I need that medicine bad."

Minutes later I am scrutinized by a man in a white jacket behind the drugstore counter. He inspects the piece of paper from Vera and then asks where I live. Without thinking, I say at Pearl's.

"I see," he says, and disappears into a back room.

When he returns he says that he has temporarily run out of that drug and that he will call when it arrives. I give him a phony tele-phone number when he asks for one and order two sundaes, one butterscotch and the other chocolate, my favorite.

Vera is extremely upset by the news that she will have to wait for her medicine and heaves the bag with the sundaes into a trash bas-ket. Squirt whimpers as I pass him on my way out of their room.

From the hall I can hear Vera shouting profanities, which she oc-casionally attaches to my name. Pearl emerges from an adjacent room clutching a dust mop and bangs on the door with its handle.

"This is a respectable house, Vera, and I won't tolerate language like that. If you want to stay here, you'd better watch your tongue and behave. You hear me?"

When there is no response, Pearl marches away seemingly un-aware of my presence. I go down to the living room hoping to find Ole Moses, but it is empty. The rest of the afternoon I entertain my-self by pretending to be Steve McQueen in *Wanted: Dead or Alive*. My imaginary prey are the teens back at Coney Island, whom I cleverly manage to capture and rough up before turning them in to the sheriff for the enormous reward.

A direct hit with a stone at a crow that is perched on a low tree limb confirms to me my prowess as a hunter. However, immediately after striking the bird, I regret my deed. Fortunately it is none the worse for my marksmanship and flies off into the glare of the young summer sun. Wings are what I would like to have more than anything else, I think. Wings to fly west. Wings to fly away like a crow from anything that causes pain and unpleasantness.

Desperate Measures

AT SUPPER PEARL OBSERVES that my father must be working late and says she will put a plate aside for him. Something tells me that it is not the demands of envelope-addressing that are keeping him. I am also disappointed by the absence of May at the table.

Vera and Squirt pick at their food in silence, Ben is still out on the road, and Ole Moses is skipping the meal because he hates macaroni and cheese, according to Pearl.

"Don't like none of that *Eye*-talian stuff," she says, mimicking him.

The lace curtains in the dining room flap violently from the sharp gusts of wind that have suddenly stirred. Pearl says something about this being the start of twister season.

"It's always a warm day. Then it gets weird like. Real still . . . eerie. Sometimes everything gets a funny straw color. Then you hear a rumble. Like a freight train coming down the tracks full throttle. All heck breaks loose then and you better get below ground or you're going to end up like Judy Garland in that wizard movie with the flying monkeys. When I was a little girl on our farm outside Decatur we got hit by a real nasty whirligig. Took our house and barn clear off their foundation but left them standing intact. Lord was watchin' over us. Luckily we were in the storm cellar, so nobody got hurt except some livestock and our dog, who got blown clear over to the next county. Eventually we got a call from a fellow over there who said he found Cider, our dog, hanging from one of his yard trees. Broke Cider's back, but he lived. Walked like a hunchback after that and never could move in a straight line either. If you called for him from the other side of the room, he'd more than likely end up in the hall or bangin' into a wall. Poor thing. Lived to be twenty-two, though, but by then he could only walk in circles."

There is a flash of light followed by a powerful clack of thunder, and everybody at the table jumps. I think God has just let out a good one. Pearl laughs nervously and says she had better listen to the radio for any reports on tornado sightings. Without uttering a word, Vera rises from the table and exits the room, leaving Squirt behind. Another crash of thunder sends him scrambling to my side.

"Nothing but the angels moving furniture," says Pearl, trying to quell his anxiety. "So don't you be scared and wet your pants. Why don't you two go play while I clear things? Stay inside, though, till this blows by."

Hailstones the size of marbles begin to pound against the house and dining room floor. Pearl makes a sharp detour to close the windows on her way to the kitchen.

"You boys make yourselves useful and check for open windows, specially the ones without screens, 'cause they're not all in yet."

As the lights flicker ominously we dash from room to room with a great sense of urgency and purpose, looking for windows to shut. By the time we return to the first floor to report our success, the weather has come full circle and we watch the dark storm clouds recede over the trees and rooftops from the front porch.

An unexpected snap of thunder startles us, and Squirt runs off. He is out of sight before I know it. I shout after him but he does not respond. After about a half hour I grow tired of waiting for my father to appear and I go hunting for Squirt. The brightness that followed the storm has dimmed and the tall, drenched grass behind the house dampens my pants as I wade through it.

"Here I am," whispers Squirt, who is huddled against the sagging wall of a decrepit shed belonging to the house next door.

"Why'd you run away?" I inquire, and he says he was scared.

I tell him that it was just thunder or, as Pearl said, angels moving furniture. Maybe farting, I add, and he smiles.

"I know," he says in a voice that is barely audible. "I was afraid my mom would see I wet my pants again. She'll whip me hard."

"Did you wet them a lot?" I ask, and when he stands I can see that he has.

"Maybe they'll dry fast," he says hopefully, but when I check the extent of the pee stain I know that's not likely.

His eyes are red and swollen from crying and his bare legs are scratched and dirty. When I suggest that he come back to the house, he protests, and I try to think of something else.

"We could light a fire and dry them that way," I offer, and instruct him to stay put while I go get some matches.

His expression has brightened by the time I return, and we set about gathering dry sticks of wood from inside the open shed and form a pile behind it so that we will not be detected. I ignite the heap, and flames begin to leap upward almost immediately. Squirt removes his shorts and underpants and I hold them over the fire with a tree branch. Everything is going fine until a cluster of drifting embers lands on the dangling clothes. Then, to make matters worse, when I attempt to shake them off, the branch snaps and Squirt's pants fall on the flames. I retrieve them as quickly as I can without burning myself, and following a cursory inspection of the garments for fire damage locate another branch and start the drying process again.

It is not long before the pee has mostly dried and Squirt is happier than I have ever seen him.

"Let's go see Ole Moses," he suggests, pulling his shorts back on. "He's on his rock making stars. See him?"

I look where Squirt is pointing and see the dark silhouette of a person sitting on top of the large rock at the far end of the field. Squirt leads the way and I notice that a hole has been burned into the seat of his pants. I know this portends disaster for him, but I cannot help laughing to myself.

Ole Moses does not acknowledge us when we reach him. He is cutting at a piece of wood with his new Swiss Army pocketknife and acts far away. Finally he notices our presence.

"What you young'ns doin' out here? Kinda near your sack time, ain't it?"

"My mom lets me stay up late," says Squirt in a bragging tone.

"Think your mom needs talkin' to, little pal. She don't seem to do right by you," observes Ole Moses.

Squirt then asks him if he has been talking to the stars, and the old man says that in fact he has, pointing his knife toward the twinkling lights.

"You see that bright one right there? The one that shines like a beautiful diamond? See it?"

"Yes," we say.

"Well, that's Mabel, my wife. That's where she went when she passed on. So I come out here and talk to her."

He moves his outstretched arm a few inches to the left.

"The one right there is little Zach, my son. He died in a fire back in 'thirty-two. But there they are. Right up there where I can always see them. Someday I'll be up there with 'em. They're all there, you know. Everybody that's ever died, that is. All the stars are souls departed, alive forever for us to see and so they can see us. Here, young fella," he says, handing Squirt a wood carving of a star. "Hold eternity in your hand. It's got special power 'cause it comes from the heavens. In fact this one here's what's called a supernova. It's the grandest of all the stars. Talk to it in the daytime when you can't see what's up there if you got somethin' gnawin' at you. It'll put you in touch with them, the spirits of the ages. Then you'll be just fine. I'll make you one too, Mitchell . . . I mean Mikey. Maybe not a supernova like Squirt's got there. Do it after I whittle one for May. Think that little gal might need one in more of a hurry."

Squirt clutches his star as if it is the most precious object in the universe, and for several minutes we maintain a quiet skyward vigil for all the glimmering immortals peering back down on us in Indiana.

Squirt breaks the silence by calling our attention to the shed. It is on fire and when Ole Moses catches sight of it he leaps to his feet and shuffles toward the scene as fast as his feet will take him. Ben and Pearl arrive at the shed at the same time, carrying buckets of water. It is not long before they have doused the flames.

As they battle the blaze I grab Squirt by the hand and we return to the house before any questions can be asked.

Demons and Rum

IT IS JUST AFTER midnight when my father creeps into our room. This I know because I have just counted the clangs of a distant church bell from my bed. Navigating the furniture in the dark is too much for him in his present condition, and he stumbles over the metal foldout chair that I use to pile my clothes on. He curses under his breath and tries to right the fallen object, but his efforts are inadequate and he soon gives up on the idea.

When he sits on the edge of the bed, I let him have it. I do not want to go anyplace with him, I say. What I want is to go back and live with my mother. She is right about him, I continue. He is a drunken, lousy bum. A son of a bitch!

My father shushes me but says nothing in his defense as he fumbles with the laces on his shoes. I expect to incur his wrath at any moment, but that does not prevent me from unloading my stored-up anger. He has let me down again, I say. He has always let everyone down—my mother, my sisters. Why is he like this? I wonder aloud. How come he breaks every promise? What makes him ruin everything?

Images of his destructive effects assert themselves in painful profusion: My mother venting her despair and frustration at him for wasting his paycheck on booze. My sisters and I huddled in the next room while they battle it out. The neighbors intervening when it gets too raucous. My mother's disconsolate sobs. Scenes like these repeated over and over again, the dominant and haunting recollections of my charred childhood. At this moment, there is no one I resent more than him.

Later when he vomits everything his system can hold into the sink, including his false teeth, whose front tooth is chipped when it hits the porcelain, my contempt for him turns to pity and concern. Wiping the putrid drool from his mouth, he manages a pathetic apology and swears that he will never touch the stuff again. He also promises that we will be on our way to the coast in a few days.

When the contents of his belly are purged, he pees long and hard into the sink, farting a few times for added effect, and then collapses on the bed next to me. I bury my face in the pillow to block the sour stench of his breath as he pats my arm affectionately. Two or three times during the night, he is up with the dry heaves and moaning and groaning. Just before dawn a measure of calm is restored to his racked body.

Between my fitful dreams I spy him in the seagull chair near the window, shining his flashlight out into the night as if he is searching for something. He navigates the beam across the tree limbs, which look like deformed arms reaching toward us from the black and horrible unknown. I have awakened on other occasions to find him probing the darkness with his Eveready. When I question him about this peculiar habit, he just says that he is checking to make sure the batteries are okay. Maybe someone is after him, I speculate, recalling my mother's saying something about two men coming to the apartment in Albany and asking his whereabouts. Gangsters maybe, or somebody else he has made unhappy.

In the dull morning light he looks beaten and repentant, often a sign that the drinking cycle has run its nasty course, and if that is the case, it has been a short one this time. A feeling of optimism is born anew in me. The golden West may yet be mine, I think, staring out the window at the tree limbs that have been made less ominous by the dawn. They gently bob and sway in the warm currents flowing around the boardinghouse.

Apprehensions

BEN HAS PROMISED to take Squirt and me with him on one of his trips, but to our disappointment today is not the day, so we occupy ourselves by playing a variety of games, most with a western theme, in the field behind the boardinghouse.

About noon my father takes a stab at shaving with the intention of putting in a few hours at the racing magazine. His hands are unsteady as he drags his razor across his ashen cheeks. We will hit the road tomorrow, he promises in a meek voice, because he will have enough dough to take us to Saint Louis, or possibly Kansas City, but forget Denver, he says. Costs too damn much to get that far. Greyhound charges too much, he complains, adding that Trailways is no better and that half the time it doesn't even go where you're headed. From the other side of the Mississippi we should get some good rides, he concludes, because there are fewer cities and more open spaces. Longer stretches between places where people go. The Great Plains, I inform him, as I study our map. Home of Matt Dillon, Doc Holliday, and Bat Masterson, and mythical towns like Dodge City and Cimarron.

From the look in my father's eyes I can tell he is thinking about something else. I deliver my stock admonition on the subject of drinking, and he tells me he has no intention of tipping the bottle. The farthest thing from his mind, he claims with labored conviction. I recite an AA adage I recall from a pamphlet at the Oxford Arms.

"You are only one drink away from a drunk," I proclaim, and he rolls his eyes and shakes his head.

Pearl gives him a cup of coffee and a deviled ham sandwich to take to work, and I accompany him to the corner, all the while rattling off other antibooze slogans I remember from the pamphlet. Squirt is waiting for me on the porch when I return. He proudly announces that since Ole Moses gave him his star he has not wet his pants once. I congratulate him but feel envy and regret when I realize I will not be around to get my own special handmade talisman. It then occurs to me to talk Squirt into giving me his, and after an impassioned appeal he reluctantly does. After all, I tell him, Ole Moses can make him another as soon as he finishes May's. That way, I point out, we will both have a magic star and we can talk with one another simply by looking at the sky, even when I am out west and he is back in Indiana. That is the clincher.

While we are sitting on the steps, a police car pulls up and two men climb out. One is in a blue uniform, and the other looks like the detectives on television. Although it is a hot, sunny day, he is wearing a trench coat and a fedora. The first thing that comes to my mind is that these are the men after my father. The ones who questioned my mother. The trackers he watches for with his flashlight at night. Is he on the lam from the law? I wonder, recalling a line from a *Dragnet* episode.

They ask if Mrs. Lange is home, and Squirt begins to whimper while I breathe a sigh of relief. The guy who looks like Joe Friday eyes him.

"She your mom, kid?" he asks, and Squirt nods.

"Why don't you take us to her, sonny," says the cop, and we all go inside.

When Pearl sees the officers, she assumes they are there because of Mr. Waller, but the detective informs her otherwise and she joins the group as it moves upstairs to Vera's room.

There is no response when the plainclothesman knocks on the door and calls for Vera. He then directs Squirt to go in and fetch his mother. However, as soon as Squirt opens the door, they follow him inside.

At the sight of the police, Vera quickly removes a pad of paper from the table and deposits it in her purse.

"I'll take that, Mrs. Lange," says the detective as he moves swiftly to her side.

Vera protests, saying that it is only her address book. Her eyes are wide with fear and confusion. The other cop begins to look around the disheveled room and while I absorb the scene from the hall, I hear liquid splattering against the floor. Squirt stands frozen in place as a small puddle forms around his feet.

"What's this about?" asks Vera as she reluctantly surrenders the pad from her purse.

"You're under arrest for falsifying official documents. Writing phony prescriptions. Forgery. You'll have to come with us, ma'am."

"You're wrong!" snaps Vera, looking like a trapped animal. "I never did nothing like that. I'm a sick woman, and my doctor has me on special medicine for the pain. He gave me those forms to get the drugs I need until he gets back from vacation."

The red blotches on Vera's chest have darkened and spread to her neck, and there is an ugly gash just beneath her right elbow. When the detective asks her about it, she explains that the medicine she takes for her disorder makes her light headed, causing her to lose her balance occasionally and slam into things.

"Kid on the medicine too?" he asks sarcastically, noting Squirt's bruises.

When he attempts to lead Vera from the room, she pushes him away.

"Take your goddamn grubby mitts off me! I'm not going anywhere. I haven't done nothing wrong!"

The uniformed cop comes up from behind her and applies a bear hug around her body, but she manages to kick his shin and break his hold. The other cop then seizes her and throws her facedown on the unmade bed, causing her dress to ride up over her waist and revealing her underpants, which appear to be bloodstained.

Pearl does her best to console Squirt as they carry his screaming mother from the room to the waiting cruiser. His small body rocks convulsively as he sobs and pleads for them to leave his mother alone. Once outside, Vera somehow manages to break free and she is halfway down the block before being apprehended and carted back to the waiting police car.

The detective informs Pearl that a social worker will come by later to get Squirt, and when she explains that this will not be necessary because she can take care of him until the whole thing is straightened out, he tells her that those are the rules.

Squirt attempts to get into the car with his mother, who tries to grab his arm, but Pearl reaches him first and pulls him back. When the car moves away, we both hold on to him, fearing that he will chase after it.

On our way back into the house, Ole Moses greets us with his midday nap still in his eyes and asks what all the ruckus is about. Pearl tells him that he has missed a good one, and he comments that some things are worth missing.

"Be great if a person could sleep right straight through all the world's woes and be wide-eyed awake for all its joys," he says, adding, "'Course you'd be asleep a heck of a lot more than you'd be awake on this sad planet, I suppose."

Pearl takes Squirt into her arms and carries him to his empty room while I remain behind to wrestle with the guilt I feel over leading the cops to his mom. I somehow know that my conversation with the druggist has brought the police here. Ole Moses does not make me feel any better when he predicts that Squirt will probably end up in one of those dreary orphanages run by people who hate and abuse kids. It occurs to me that Mrs. Lange did not exactly treat her son with motherly love, so life might not change all that much for him in the care of mean strangers.

Taken Away

PEARL HAS GATHERED SOME of Squirt's things and placed them in a suitcase whose clasps are badly broken. She locates some twine and ties it around the dilapidated Samsonite.

"How can anybody take a quality travelin' case and wreck it like this? You know what a person has to do to cause this much damage? It's beyond my comprehension," she complains, tying the final knot in the twine.

Not long after Squirt's mother is taken away, someone calls and informs Pearl that a Miss Eisman from Juvenile Services will be by to collect him in a couple of hours. Again Pearl asks that Squirt be allowed to remain at the boardinghouse until his mother is released from jail, but she is told that it's not possible by the person on the other end of the receiver.

"Them and their darn rules," she says, hanging up the phone. "They don't know what's best for him."

When the doorbell sounds, Squirt grabs ahold of her waist as if he were about to be dragged off by the Creature from the Black Lagoon.

"You stay here with Mitch . . . er, Michael, sugar. Don't worry, I'll see who it is and make sure everything is okay," says Pearl, cupping Squirt's flushed cheeks in her hands.

He reluctantly follows her orders but not without significant protest. To him, she has become his protector, his brave and stalwart auntie Pearl, who will not give up her child without a bloody fight. Why, I wonder, did my mother not fight as hard to keep me? Perhaps I was less deserving of such an all-out effort. I take the opportunity to give back his carved star and reiterate Ole Moses' words about its being filled with heavenly powers and how he does not have to be afraid of anything as long as he has it.

This helps and when Pearl returns and reports that it is the lady sent to collect him, Squirt is not quite as adamant about staying. Still he weeps loudly when he is led to the waiting stranger.

Pearl makes a last-ditch effort to keep him, and to add weight to her appeal Squirt promises that he will not wet his pants ever again if he can remain at the boardinghouse. While these words have a visible impact on the young woman, she explains that it is not her decision and that she has been directed to pick up the young man, as she calls him, and take him to the juvenile center for appropriate processing.

We bid good-bye to Squirt and he is loaded into the backseat of a black Ford station wagon. When the car turns the corner at the end of the block, Pearl lets out a deep sigh and shakes her head.

"Poor little thing. Probably never see him again. What a way to spend the first five years of your life on this earth. Lord have mercy on him."

The next day I imagine Pearl paraphrasing this lament on my behalf when addressing our sudden disappearance and the rapidly shrinking population at the boardinghouse.

PART III
INDIANAPOLIS TO DENVER
(1,101 Miles)

Through the Gate

SAINT LOUIS IS THE true gateway to the West, my father tells me, attempting to placate my disappointment. We do not have enough money to buy tickets as far as Kansas City, and I renew my contention that if he had not wasted cash on booze we would have. He says that is a stupid idea and that we will catch a ride there easily enough anyway. I know the wide-open plains will not begin in earnest until we are a lot farther beyond the Missouri River. To me these arid flatlands, depicted in beige on our road map of the United States and in gray in television westerns, represent the first genuine evidence of the real West, and I make a pact with myself to go it alone if it takes much longer to reach my elusive promised land.

Before Pearl has a chance to spot us we are out of the boarding-house and on our way to the bus depot. I am bothered by what she may think when she discovers we have skipped out on her. All my father has to say about leaving is that he was getting writer's cramp from addressing all those dumb envelopes. They could train a monkey to do that job in fifteen minutes, he comments with a sneer in his voice.

At the Greyhound station we stay clear of the Travelers Aid desk in case Pearl's friend happens to be on duty. Shortly past seven o'clock we climb aboard a double-deck Scenicruiser for our south-westerly jaunt. The smell of the big bus is sweet perfume to me. The mixture of exhaust fumes with the scent of the elements that form the interior cabin makes me giddy. This is the fragrance of travel and movement and a balm to my young and restless soul.

The countryside we cross gives a hint of what lies ahead. It is level with the horizon in places and dotted with lonely farmhouses, but there are still thick clusters of leafy trees that serve as an unpleasant reminder to me of the overfoliated East. It is the rugged and dusty desolation that my heart yearns for, not flowers, shrubs, and trees.

We arrive in Saint Louis by early afternoon and begin scouting for a Catholic church. Priests always live next door in rectories, unlike in other religious denominations, observes my father, who plans to relate his California scenario to a sympathetic one in the hope that cash may be raised to get us on our way again. I am coached to say nothing. Should I be asked any questions, I am simply to echo what my father has been saying.

"You could find a place to sell blood," I suggest, and he ignores me.

Not far from the bus station, we see a steeple with a crucifix that turns out to be the city's Catholic cathedral. A housekeeper, whose heavy accent reminds me of Bela Lugosi's, answers the door to the rectory and takes us into a richly furnished study with floor-to-ceiling bookshelves and large portraits of winged saints with luminous halos. It is here that we are to await the arrival of someone she softly and reverently refers to as the monsignor.

When we are alone my father reminds me to keep my mouth closed, and just before the door swings open he throws me the V sign, which I have seen Winston Churchill use in old Movietone newsreels.

A white-haired priest with a ruby complexion and a kindly smile introduces himself as Father Finn. My father gives our names, and to provide additional weight to his claim that we are who we say we are, he shows the priest his Social Security card and the gray photostatic copy of his army discharge, which is held together with strips of clear adhesive tape that have yellowed with age.

The priest nods without really inspecting the documents and waves to us to return to our seats. My father's voice quavers slightly as he conveys our dilemma, and I wonder if the priest possesses special powers to detect lies and whether fibbing to a monsignor is worse than fibbing to a normal priest. Maybe that is what has my father quaking, I think, and observe that his gaze is occasionally fixed on the painting just behind the monsignor, which depicts the suffering and melancholy face of Christ as he hangs on the Cross.

The smiling priest lets my father complete his tale and then he asks how I am doing. There is no hint of suspicion or doubt in his demeanor, only warmth and kindness, which intensify my discomfort over our deceiving him. I say that I am okay and nothing more and he comments that I look a little on the thin side. My father seizes the opportunity to reemphasize our plight.

"Things have been a bit tough lately. I don't mind going without, but it really bothers me when he has to, because he's only a child," he says with a look on his face that reminds me of the painting on the wall.

"What can I do for you?" asks the amiable monsignor, leaning forward in his high-backed leather chair, and my father says if there was just some way to get enough money to reach the West Coast everything would be all right.

"Well, there might be a way we could use you around here. Do you know how to reupholster furniture? That is, cover it with fabric? We lost our man for that job."

This question leaves my father at a momentary loss for words because he has not anticipated being offered actual work, let alone this kind of job, by the priest. It was his assumption that he would simply be handed a few bucks and that would be that. He has never reupholstered a thing in his life, but rather than risk getting nothing he says he has covered a few things.

The monsignor is delighted to hear this and says he will make arrangements for us to stay in a small neighborhood hotel and eat at a nearby restaurant. It is in the very room in which we are seated that my father is to ply his newfound upholstering skills. The fabric and tools for the project are stored in a closet and when the priest displays them to my father he acts as if they are familiar objects.

"Looks good," he says with a confident nod while pretending to carefully inspect the materials. "Yeah, they'll do the job, all right."

I am wondering how he is going to extricate himself from this predicament and at the same time get us the money we need to resume our trip.

After making the necessary phone calls to secure our food and lodging, the priest instructs my father to return first thing in the morning to begin work on the chair.

"It has a couple of small holes in it, so now is the time to cover it before it gets worse," observes the priest, who admits to dropping the lighted contents of his pipe on it more than once.

I am to serve as my father's special assistant, he says, and if I like I can join a catechism class that meets in the afternoon.

"You've made your first Holy Communion, haven't you?" he asks, and I say that I have, my father adding that the one thing he has tried to do despite all the adversity in his life—his war injury, the layoffs, and so on—is to keep up his children's religious education.

He does not tell the good priest that he is really a lapsed Episcopalian, who resents my mother's insistence that her children be brought up as Catholics, a religion of spicks and guineas and those rum-running Irish Kennedys, he calls it, among other even less flattering things.

On our way out of the monsignor's study I expect my father to make a last-ditch bid for some cash, especially since we are down to change after purchasing bus tickets to Saint Louis and because his cigarette supply is rapidly dwindling, but he does not.

Out on the street I criticize his handling of the situation, particularly his claim that he can reupholster furniture.

"What happens if he finds out? He can have us put in jail," I contend.

My father says not to worry about that because he has no intention of going back. His next idea involves calling my mother collect to see if she can wire us some money. Later in the day, when he has built up the courage, he puts his scheme into action from a phone booth outside of our hotel. Despite the fact that my father will not be returning to the rectory, we check in to the hotel the priest has found for us.

I can tell from my father's expression that my mother is throwing a fit. She has not heard from us in weeks. All I can hear are my father's words, but I can easily imagine what my mother is saying.

"Saint Louis! What are you doing there? I'm getting the cops after you. I swear to God! You didn't say anything about leaving Albany California! Why? I want him back here now, damn it! Yes, I'll get the money for his ticket somewhere, maybe my father," says my mother, and my father tells her to keep quiet about this to old Mac.

The mere mention of my grandfather makes my father's face turn bright red. He will never forgive Mac for punching him in the nose during one of his drunken disputes with my mother. I am sure the blow is at least partially responsible for the vastness of his snout, a term my father uses to describe other people's large noses. It has disfigured his looks and injured his pride, and that is why my father hates my grandfather and everyone Irish, I figure.

"You better send him back here!" shouts my mother, loud enough for me to hear her voice over the phone. "If you don't, I'll have the police and my father come after you. I have legal custody, don't forget. Has he been eating? Jesus, Curt, he's just a child. I should never have let you talk me into letting him live with you again. I'm so naive. How could you do this?"

My father tells her not to cry, that everything will be okay, and to send the money care of the Western Union in Saint Louis as soon as possible. She wants to talk to me, he says, passing me the phone and putting his butt-stained index finger over his lips as a signal for me to say nothing about our true plans.

"Hello, honey. Are you okay? I'm going to send the money so that you can come home, all right? Make sure your father puts you on the bus, and don't talk to strangers. Only the driver, okay? I'll see you soon. Pam and Claudia miss you."

My mother puts my sisters on the line and they repeat her statement about missing me. Pamela tells me she still has the lucky rabbit-foot I gave her before leaving. This may be why things haven't gone so great for us, I speculate. Being without that special amulet has probably made us more susceptible to bad fortune. Despite this disturbing thought, it is good to hear their voices and I feel a little like a celebrity because of all the attention. Guilt is something else I feel because I know we are lying to them about my returning.

My father signs off by reiterating his request that my mother send the money right away and then vowing to send me home. Perhaps experiencing some guilt later himself, he asks if I would like to go back to Albany but immediately follows his inquiry with the observation that the dough being wired will probably buy two tickets to Kansas City or maybe farther. I opt for the bus tickets west.

The money order arrives later that evening and I insist that we purchase the bus tickets before returning to the hotel for the night. I am not taking any chances. On the way to our room we stop at a drugstore to restock my father's cigarette supply and I buy a postcard featuring a Mississippi riverboat captioned "Up the river with a paddle," which I might send to my mother.

Heartland

MISSOURI HAS MORE HILLS and trees than I expect, although it is hard to tell much because we cross the state in the dark. My father's strategy involves hanging around Saint Louis all the next day and most of the evening in order to catch a bus that leaves around midnight. This gives us a roof over our heads for the night, getting us to Kansas City around dawn with a full day to hitch a ride. With a twenty-five-cent rental pillow nestled under my head, a legitimate luxury, I sleep most of the way.

The Kansas City streets are quiet when we arrive at daybreak. To me it looks like any other town. It is devoid of any signs that would indicate it is on the very threshold of the great western territory. A check of our crinkled map reveals that we have to cross a Missouri River bridge to get to the most advantageous point for hitchhiking. At least this is what my father deduces, restating the key points of his thesis on catching rides. A trek of a couple of miles lies ahead, and it reminds me of crossing the Hudson.

As it turns out, the road we need runs straight through the city and across the bridge, so we can thumb for a ride as we walk. Traffic is scarce, but within ten minutes we catch a ride in a rusty Dodge pickup truck bound for Topeka.

The Missouri River is wide and possesses the consistency and color of cocoa, and I know from my Rand McNally studies that it stretches through the Dakotas to within miles of the Montana border. It would be wonderful to ride a boat the entire length. I picture the two of us floating along unimpaired by earthly roadblocks, the current gently carrying us to our destination.

Halfway across the bridge a sign welcomes us to Kansas, the Sunflower State. I am immediately filled with a sense of attainment. This is the beginning of the West, where cattlemen battled angry Indians and one another. The land of the brave pioneers and homesteaders, of stagecoaches and the Pony Express, of Hopalong Cassidy and Geronimo. The true frontier and where Armour meats are processed, according to a giant billboard that momentarily blocks our view of the distance.

Another ride takes us still deeper into what a different sign calls the HEART OF THE HEARTLAND. Around noon we are standing with our thumbs outstretched at a point nearly halfway across the state, on the outskirts of a town named Salina. From here the land climbs until it reaches the foothills of the Rocky Mountains. At that point it will have risen a mile above sea level, yet there is no hint of ascent. The earth has flattened to where it is possible to see a hundred miles, I estimate. There are few objects to obstruct the view. It is like standing on the forehead of the world. Trees have become rare and when they do appear they form protective barriers around solitary farmhouses and barns—what I prefer to think of as ranches. Mammoth grain silos, looking like displaced skyscrapers, stand on the cusp of the remote horizon, so far away . . . so enticingly far away. I concentrate my gaze on the sights ahead, where the change in topography is most pleasing to me. There is no turning back now. My addiction to this direction is absolute, my love of westward motion sublime. This is where the theme from *The Magnificent Seven* begins to assume greater legitimacy to me.

My father is less enamored of the stark scenery. It does not have the same intoxicating effect on him. He is worried that the growing desolation will result in hardship.

"Jesus, there's not much out here," moans my father with an edginess in his voice as he surveys the surrounding emptiness. "This damn sun will get to you too," he adds, placing his hand over his sable eyebrows.

We consult our map again to see what decent-size towns lie ahead and conclude that Hays is the largest between us and Denver. It should be our destination for the day, he says, but I balk at this, since it is less than a hundred miles away and it is barely afternoon.

"There's nine hours left before it gets dark," I protest, but my father is already anticipating the worst.

"We could be stuck out here in the middle of nothing for the night. Let's just see what happens. Don't start yapping again, for God's sake."

In the thick of our debate a car pulls over and honks at us. It has a West Virginia license plate, which is good. We are learning that catching a ride from a car with in-state markers usually means a local run, whereas out-of-state cars are often headed beyond state lines. At least that is the theory we have begun to formulate. This one is not, however. The driver says that he and his family are going down the road to WaKeeney to hook up with a traveling carnival there. No matter, it is a good lift, around 150 miles, I quickly calculate, but my father indicates that although we are going all the way to the West Coast, we are stopping in Hays for the night.

"No problem, mister," says the driver, whose blond hair is cut into a smooth flattop with sideburns that drop well below his earlobes. "Hop aboard. Make room, y'all."

I climb in back, where there are two small children, a boy and a girl roughly the age of my sisters. My father gets into the front seat next to a woman whose stomach sticks out like she is hiding a watermelon under her clothes.

"Y'all from back east, ain'tcha?" she asks, turning to me and smiling. "Kin tell from the way y'all sound yer words out. Bet we sound kinda funny to y'all too."

One of her teeth is missing from the front of her mouth and the rest are uneven and discolored, but her face is pretty. She has enormous green eyes, which are called hazel, like mine, my mother's, and

Pamela's. Claudia's and my father's eyes are more yellow gray than anything, although my father dislikes that description, claiming his are hazel too. When I teased him once by saying that his are more the color of pee than of sea, he became highly irritated and accused me of being a little snot.

"You're just like your old lady. She never has anything good to say about me either," he added, and before I could respond he instructed me to keep my fresh trap shut.

He is committed to the notion that his eyes are like mine and is not about to be dissuaded. It is important to him for reasons that I do not fully appreciate.

"We're the Leaches from Ripley, WV. I'm Tom and this here's my wife, Belly."

"It's Belle. Don't listen to silly here," protests his wife with a chuckle that sounds like a horse snorting.

"She's about to drop me a new young'n," continues Tom, "so Belly is what I call her. Fit too, don't it? Them in back with your boy is Justice and Blanche. Named the girl child after my aunt, and I named the boy there Justice after my poor old uncle who never got none. Ain't gonna tell ya why he din't git none but was in jail mosta his sorry life."

My father introduces us and gives a brief account of how we happen to be thumbing in central Kansas, as cheese sandwiches are passed around. In this version of the story my mother is sick in an Albany hospital with a burst appendix, and we are on our way to California to raise money to pay the medical bills—since my father got laid off from his hotel job—and send for her and my sisters, who are staying with a relative during this trying time.

"No shit!" exclaims Tom. "That sure be a bad bit of luck, partner."

Playing it up, my father says we have had a lot of that lately. I am not sure why he has chosen to alter the yarn, but the Leaches are very sympathetic and Belly offers us another sandwich to split between us. Tom spits tobacco into a Dixie cup he keeps in his left hand and gulps down the sandwich his wife has unwrapped from newspaper for him. With his mouth stuffed he observes that nothing is worse than losing your health.

"Kin have all the gold in the world, but ya ain't got flea shit if yer sickly," he says, spraying pieces of cheese, bread, and chewing tobacco all over the dashboard and windshield.

The Leach children eat their lunch quietly without taking their eyes off me once. When I smile at them they smile back, and the little girl hides behind her brother's shoulder the same way Pamela takes refuge behind mine.

"Got folks in Hays, Curt?" asks Belly, who balances her lunch on her extended midsection.

My father explains that he is going to try to get someone to put us up for the night so we can hit the road good and early in the morning for Denver. There, he says, he will probably grab some kind of work to make money for the rest of the trip.

"Don't want to get stranded on the road out here at night with the kid," says my father.

I resent his using me as an excuse to cut our travel short and I suggest that we go as far as WaKeeney and try to get a ride from there. My father makes light of this suggestion, saying that kids never worry about the consequences in life. Tom proposes that we join up with the carnival like they are, claiming that it always needs help and that the pay is good.

"Bet ya kin get work. Be happy ta ask fer ya. Know the boss. They feed ya, and ya kin find a place to bed down. Whar gonna go with it up to Nebraska, around Holdrege. Few weeks and ya got yerself a pretty good piece of change," says Tom, shaking the remainder of a Skoal tin into the depths of his jaw.

The idea of working for a carnival sounds pretty good to me even if it will slow down our westward progress, but my father is not keen on it. However, he does agree to ride as far as WaKeeney after continued pressure from me.

Meanwhile the cheese sandwich has hit my stomach with a thud, causing me painful cramps and gusts of gas, which I try my best to hold inside but cannot. Each time the air seeps out of me, my two backseat companions make funny faces and giggle. Fortunately the emissions do not have the range or potency to carry them to the front of the car, where my father and the Leaches carry on an animated conversation. This is the likely consequence of unmoved bowels, I conclude, imagining a grotesque backup in my lower guts. How long can I contain everything I eat without bursting? I wonder.

West of Hays we pass a sign that reads SEE THE WORLD'S LARGEST HERD OF BUFFALO and COLD DRINKS. We stop for a soda but do not see any buffalo because it costs fifty cents per person, including children, to get beyond a tall fortresslike barrier to where they purportedly roam. Back in the car, Tom claims that they probably were not the real thing anyway.

"Buncha Herefords and Angus covered in buffalo skins, betcha."

I disagree, noting that the Great Plains serves as home for most of the country's buffalo population.

"That so? Yer a pretty smart lil fella," says Belly.

"Too smart sometimes. Thinks he should be on the radio and he's not even twelve yet," observes my father, who clearly has misgivings about what awaits us up ahead.

We reach the dusty carnival grounds in WaKeeney as the sun begins to peek beneath the windshield visors.

WaKeeney Carny

MOUNDS OF WOODEN planks and brown canvas are being un-
loaded from trucks in a field just outside of the town. When Tom
catches sight of the BRIAR BROTHERS sign, emblazoned with colorful balloons, confetti, and streamers, he shouts, "Welcome home,
critters!"

This is the third summer the Leaches have worked the carnival,
one of several things we learn about them during our long ride. Another is that Belly is Tom's first wife, although the children are his
from two other relationships back in West Virginia.

"Different mamas," says Belly, patting her pregnancy. "But love
those two little ones like they come from my own body," she adds,
looking back affectionately at Justice and Blanche.

"Plant the seed and harvest the crop," Tom says good-humoredly.

"Well, ya ain't harvestin' this'n, so yer gonna have to keep on
plowin'," replies Belly in an equally upbeat tone, and they both
laugh loudly.

"Honey, you know plowin's my specialty," responds Tom, who
swings the car up to a trailer marked OFFICE and then tells us to wait
while he talks to Mr. Briar about our joining up.

Justice and Blanche leap from the car and run excitedly toward
a heavyset woman emerging from around the side of the trailer.

"Mrs. Briar," shouts Belly, attempting to maneuver her body
from the front seat.

They embrace and Mrs. Briar says something about Belly forgetting to wipe off the toilet seat as she examines the younger woman's bulging middle.

When Tom comes out of the trailer he says, "Yer in. Both you and the boy. Now let's help 'em set up the joints."

He explains to us that *joints* is carny talk for the game and concession stands, and for the next couple of hours we watch the construction more than contribute to it. Amazingly a small town is erected before the sun has slipped over the horizon.

In the chow line, which is set up in a tent, we are introduced to Mr. Briar, who is as plump and friendly as his wife. Reading from a clipboard in his hand, he tells us what joints to work. I am assigned to Can the Cats and my father will be manning the Fishbowl.

We can sack out in the cab of the Gyrorama truck, he says, until something better can be figured out. My excitement has been building since we arrived. The idea of working for a traveling carnival in the middle of the wide-open spaces of western Kansas is perfectly exquisite to me and almost more than I can handle, and I am about to boil over from the extreme pleasure of it all.

The person who operates the Can the Cats joint is not too thrilled when Mr. Briar introduces me as his new sidekick.

"Lloyd, meet Mikey. Mikey, meet Lloyd," says Mr. Briar without making eye contact with the carny.

I extend my hand but Lloyd shoots me a "get lost" look, saying that he does not need any help and sure as hell does not have time to baby-sit. Briar tells him to put a lid on it, that I will be a good distraction, and then he walks off. Lloyd's hammering of the countertop with his fist deepens my apprehension.

"Get behind here, kid, and keep your friggin' eyes off my foot. You got that?"

Of course my eyes immediately go to his foot, which rests on a long wooden bar running the width of the countertop.

"Now what'd I just say? You deaf, sonny?" growls Lloyd, once again pounding at the countertop.

The object of the game is to knock down three stuffed cats with three balls in order to win a look-alike stuffed cat. My job is to right the cats after they have been flattened, and I have a vague suspicion that Lloyd can make toppling the felines more difficult by moving his foot.

From the Cats joint I have a clear view of my father across the carnival's main fairway. He is standing in front of a large tank made to look like a fishbowl and is holding a bamboo fishing pole and sporting a huge straw hat that sits on his narrow head like an umbrella. The flashing neon sign above him reads FISHBOWL. CATCH A FISH AND WIN A DISH! The back wall is covered with colorful plates of all shapes and sizes. My father waves, shakes his head in mock disgust, and sticks out his upper plate. This time I laugh because he looks even more ridiculous than he usually does performing his false-teeth trick. The straw hat and fishing pole definitely heighten the effect.

The brightly illuminated carnival grounds are soon thick with people, whom Lloyd refers to as hayseeds and suckers. The crowd consists primarily of farmers or ranchers and their families, I deduce, and this clearly is a big event in their lives.

Can the Cats is located next to the carousel, whose calliope music is nearly deafening. Several people have tried and failed to knock over the cats, and in particular one unaccompanied young man dressed in denim coveralls has invested a load of quarters in an attempt to do so. His frustration mounts with each successive shot, which for all the world seems to be on the mark, but Lloyd collects his money with utter indifference to his plight. At one point as I am restoring a half-downed cat to its upright position I notice a metal rod pressed against the base of the cats, clearly locking them in place.

My eyes just naturally fall on Lloyd's foot when I turn around, and this catches the contestant's attention.

"Hey, what's under there?" he asks Lloyd, who fires me a murderous glance.

"If you want to play again, it's a quarter, buddy," he responds, but the young man's suspicion is now full-blown.

"What the hell you doin' under there? You been cheatin' me, ain't you? Buncha rotten gypsy crooks! I want my money back or I'm gettin' the sheriff."

"Move along, barnshit, or I'll move you myself," spits Lloyd, and I see his hand drift down to a bat under the counter.

Mr. Briar arrives just in time to prevent Lloyd from following through on his threat. Both sides tell their story, and the carnival owner directs Lloyd to give back his money, all the while claiming that his carnival is as honest as a Baptist church bazaar.

"We don't cheat our customers, mister," he says, and for good measure he throws in a stuffed animal and a ticket for the carousel.

Peace is restored and the placated customer heads off in the direction of the fried-dough stand. When he is out of earshot I am accused by Lloyd of causing all the trouble.

"Can't keep his goddamn eyes off the friggin' bar," he protests to Briar, and I am reassigned to a joint called Spot the Dot, which involves pitching a nickel onto a table and covering one of the dozens of small colored circles painted on it. Each color represents a different cash prize, ranging from a quarter to five dollars. I count three five-dollar dots, which are about the size of the nickels being tossed, making it all but impossible to fully cover them and win.

I am quickly coached on what to do and say by the woman running the game, and in no time I am shouting the virtues of Spot the Dot along with her. Soon there is a throng of people flinging coins, and I feel I have the knack of it.

Not one person has succeeded in covering a single dot in the first hour that I work the game, but the crowd has swollen nonetheless.

"You got a talent for this, young man," I am told by my companion, who says her real name is Gertrude but that her friends call her Ruby. She does not explain why and I figure it must have to do with her bright red hair, which fans out from the back of her head like a peacock's feathers. I should call her Ruby too, she says, and then tells me to pocket a dollar for every three I take in.

"Just don't let Old Man Briar catch you. Everybody does the same thing. It's the only way you make any real money around here," she says, scanning the area.

When I pocket my first dollar I feel a mix of elation and guilt. A few dollars later I feel only exhilaration. Every so often I catch a glimpse of my father standing in his silly outfit. Fishbowl apparently is not a big attraction to Kansas ranchers and farmers, but maybe this has to do with his lack of what Ruby terms barkmanship, I surmise.

"You gotta excite the people, not just stand there like you're waitin' for a train. It takes a real gift to draw and hold a crowd. You got barkmanship in your bones, honey child," she tells me with great conviction.

Maybe I should make a career of this, she proposes, and I think, What would be better than to work for a carnival that roams the northern plains in the summer and the southwestern desert in the winter? Not much, I figure, but I can tell from my father's plaintive expression that this is not the life he has fantasized.

Slick Young Man

COLORED COWBOYS! I didn't think such a thing existed, but here they are, resplendent in their leather chaps, boots, Stetsons, and rhinestone shirts, tossing nickels. No movie or television show has prepared me for this sight and I wonder if they are a special Briar Brothers attraction: "World's Only Negro Cowpokes!"

"Ain't they somethin'? May be with the rodeo that pulls in day after tomorrow," comments Ruby.

"Rodeo?" I ask, and she says the carnival always hooks up with the county rodeo because it makes for better business.

"Two attractions 'stead of just one. Think there's a slew of folk here now, just wait. Place is butt-to-butt. First time I ever seen any coons here, though, cowboys or otherwise."

Later when Ruby mentions the colored cowboys to Mr. Briar, he says they are buffalo soldiers.

"Always been a few of them since they rode cavalry back in the eighteen-hundreds. Some of the best bull and bronco riders you ever seen too," he tells her.

While he is clearing out the cashbox to make more room, Ruby comments that she cannot cotton to the notion of coloreds on horseback trying to be Randolph Scott.

"Better left to strummin' the banjo and workin' the farm. Shouldn't try being something they ain't."

"Saw one shoot a Winchester better than any white guy. Could pick off a fly at two hundred yards," replies Briar, who then leaves.

I am relieved when he is gone because I fear he will notice the bulge of dollar bills in my pants pocket. Ruby laughs and tells me that maybe I am getting too greedy.

"'Sides, you shouldn't jam 'em all in one pocket. Spread 'em round some. Hey, I counted mine out and got over thirty dollars. More than you, I betcha. So I guess I'm the greedy one," she says, patting the hip pockets of her skirt.

When I glimpse over at my father, he is awarding a stuffed fish to one of the buffalo soldiers. Ruby notices and comments that one thing those people know how to do best is bait a line. She laughs when another colored cowboy hands my father a cigarette.

"Looks like your daddy can bait a line himself," she observes, handing a customer a roll of nickels.

The crowd thins out around midnight, and Mr. Briar collects the last batch of cash and says to close down the joints until tomorrow. He says he has been watching me, and my heart pounds.

"You're a pretty slick young man. I seen what you were doing."

I am about to make a full confession and throw myself at his mercy, when he comments that I have a future in the carnival business if I want one.

"You got the callin', son," he says, beaming at me, and Ruby adds that she has not seen one quite like me at such a tender age.

Briar repeats his praise of me when my father approaches.

"You got a real little barker here, Curt. Gonna make a heap of greenbacks."

As he heads off to the next joint, Briar reminds us that we are to bunk in the Gyrorama truck, adding that tomorrow he will find a more suitable place for the rising star of the Briar Brothers carnival.

"Maybe the boy will let you bunk with him, Curt," he jokes as he crosses the dirt path to the Lion Safari joint, which lets patrons shoot at cutouts of wild animals with Daisy BB guns.

When we are in the truck, I remove the dollar bills from my pockets and my father has a coughing fit.

"Where did you get all that? You steal it? Jesus, these carnies are a rough bunch. They'll break your neck if they find out you robbed them."

"I didn't steal it," I protest. "Not exactly. That lady, Ruby, told me everybody does it. Some for them and some for you. Every three dollars you take in, you put one in your own pocket, she says. Didn't anyone tell you?" I ask, and the answer is obvious.

I count out twenty-two dollars and my father says that it should easily get us to Denver. We spend the balance of the night trying our best to get comfortable on the torn and worn-out truck seat, and before the sun is up we slip away from the carnival grounds and walk into town, looking for the bus station. My career as a carnival barker is over. Any sense of loss I feel, though, is overshadowed by the lure of the road.

The store with a Greyhound sign painted on its window is closed when we reach it, but a schedule taped to its door indicates a Denver-bound bus is due at 6:45 A.M. Next stop, the Rocky Mountain time zone, I think jubilantly.

"Westward ho the wagons!" I shout, and my father tells me to pipe down so we do not draw unwanted attention and end up back at the carnival in chains.

The Greyhound is on time and to my joy the front seat is empty. I can think of nothing better than this at the moment. It is the beginning of a great day. In less than two hours, after passing through other dusty prairie towns like Quinter, Grainfield, Oakley, Colby, Brewster, Goodland, and Kanorado, I will be in my first honest-to-God western state, with only Utah and Nevada separating me from the Pacific Ocean.

"Hi-yo Silver, away!" I whisper to myself, and begin humming the theme from *The Magnificent Seven* as the bus moves down WaKeeney's deserted main drag.

Denver Daze

WE HAVE STALLED in the Mile High City. Many weeks have passed because my father has lost his taste for thumbing rides and has taken a job as an elevator operator at the Hotel Ames. The strategy behind this layover is to gather enough money to reach Los Angeles in one unbroken leap, but it is almost Labor Day and we have been unable to put aside a cent.

Things cost money, my father snaps when I complain about our lack of progress. The cost of our efficiency room, or light housekeeping studio apartment as it is more glamorously called, off Colfax Avenue and other basic living expenses take up my father's twenty-nine-dollar-a-week paycheck and the occasional tips he earns. We live in the hope that he will get to bellhop a couple of days a week as the manager has promised.

"A few days on the floor and we'll have plenty for tickets. Those guys do okay. That's why they hold on to those gigs. Maybe something will open up at the Brown Palace. They rake it in there."

He has canvassed other hotels for a better-paying job but nothing has panned out. I pass my days wandering the city and going to quarter movie matinees when I have the price of admission. The plan now is for me to attend school when it begins and continue until we are able to get back on the road. So I am registered in the sixth grade at a school in our district. My father has to promise the assistant principal that he will send for my transcripts.

"Why do they need records, for Christ's sakes?" he complains later. "You're only a kid. What do they think that place is, Harvard or something?"

Our landlord, Mr. Miller, tells me to drop down to his apartment anytime. He has a television, so this sounds good to me. My father thinks he is a little weird, but he likes him anyway because Mr. Miller does not press for the rent if it is a few days late.

I take him up on his offer a couple of weeks later when my father is put on the 3 to 11 P.M. shift at the hotel. My loneliness and boredom reach a peak in the evenings when it gets too dark to be outside. Other than a small crystal radio receiver shaped like a rocket ship that we purchase for ninety-nine cents at a drugstore, there is nothing to entertain me in our room, whose only window faces a vacant and crumbling building almost within touching distance.

Mr. Miller is surprised to see me at his door and I hope he really meant what he said about my coming down. My doubts are dispelled when he breaks into a broad smile and tells me that I am just in time for *Have Gun Will Travel* and a scoop of coffee ice cream. His living room is crowded with old furniture and made all the more cramped by a hospital bed positioned against a wall. On it lies the frail and depleted frame of his ancient and sickly mother, who is sleeping or maybe unconscious, even dead, I think.

"Mother's pretty ill. She sleeps all the time, but when she's awake she loves to watch the television. Especially the soap operas. *The Guiding Light* is her favorite. That's why her bed is in here. It wouldn't fit through the door to her bedroom anyway, not without taking it all apart, so we set it up in the living room. Works fine that way."

Seeing my curiosity, he adds, "Don't worry, she doesn't have anything you can catch, and you don't have to be quiet either. She sleeps through everything, and even when she's awake she's pretty deaf. I check her pulse every so often to make sure she's still around. She has lung and kidney problems. Smoked three packs of Lucky Strikes a day for nearly sixty years. She smokes in her dreams now. You'll probably see her do it. Kind of funny, actually. She puts an in-

visible cig in her mouth and lights it up. Inhales just like she is drawing actual smoke. After a couple of puffs she starts coughing and
wheezing, and that usually wakes her up. Then she asks for a real
cigarette, which she can't have."

Mr. Miller has the same face as his mother, I determine. Both
have small, dainty noses and almond-shaped eyes that are set wide
apart. Their lips consist of thin brownish lines that look penciled
onto their long faces. Mrs. Miller has few wrinkles but looks time-
worn just the same and I figure that she must have been about my
father's age when she had her son too. I think people so old shouldn't
have kids, especially young ones they can't take care of.

I can call him by his first name, he says, which is Web, short for
Webster. On the television, Richard Boone, known as Paladin, is
saving a rancher's family from a band of rowdy cattle rustlers led by
the walleyed character actor Jack Elam. One outlaw is so crippled
by the sight of Boone's acne-scarred face and cold, reptilian eyes that
he reminds me of a shocked wildebeest I saw attacked by a lion in
a jungle movie. The bad guy's life is spared, however, courtesy of the
civilized gunfighter, whose business card is adorned with a chess
piece.

During the closing credits there is a knock on the door and it
turns out to be my father. Right away I detect a slight slur in his
speech when he asks Web if he has seen me.

"Yeah, he's here. Come on in. We're watching TV."

Remaining at the door, my father explains how the elevator at
the Ames broke down, so he got off early, but he does not care to
watch the radio—*television* is a word he seems unwilling or unable
to assimilate—and wants me to come out.

My anger mounts on the way to our third-floor room, and before we reach it I pull out the stops, accusing him once more of
spoiling everything by drinking. Of course he denies this, and I am
somewhat relieved to see that he has barely penetrated the forward
edge of a drunk.

Once inside our room, I search for a liquor bottle and am

incensed when he laughs and says I would make a good blood-hound. There is nothing to be found, however, and I desperately hope that his drinking will go no further than this early stage. Maybe I will get lucky again.

No matter how little he has consumed, booze loosens his tongue. It is the only time he speaks about his past, the forty years of his life before I entered the scene. As is typical during the early rounds of a bout with the bottle, he talks about some of the people and events of his other life, as I tend to think of it. I have heard most of his accounts before. There have been many opportunities. Among the most familiar is his story about his father, my grandfather, which he recounts to my less-than-enthusiastic reception.

"He was something, I tell you. Driven. Too driven for his own good and everyone else's. He was on Wall Street. Made a bundle of dough, then lost it all in the crash. But he made most of it back. Helped build Aladdin City down in Florida. The guy had a real head on his shoulders when it came to business. Knew where to make a buck. There's a plaque with his name on it down there somewhere. I think in Coral Gables. Maybe we'll get down there to check it out. The pressures got to him though. He dropped dead getting out of his limo in front of a bank in Worcester when he was only fifty-six. Never had much time for me. Wasn't around like I am with you. I hated his second wife. She had platinum blond hair like Jean Harlow, and those skinny eyebrows too, and she was a real miserable woman. Never liked me, and I never liked her. She was a real dill, that one. A pisser from the word *go*. I spent most of my time on the train between my mother's place in Westwood and my father's house in the city. Haven't the slightest idea what he saw in her, except that hair. It was pretty, all right. She could be nasty. I don't know if he ever saw that side of her, but I did. She was sly. One time, when he was away on business, Millie—that was her name—got tight and chased me around the house with a pair of scissors. I left for good that time. When my father died she got everything. I lost track of where she is, but I think she's still alive. She wasn't a lot older than me. My old man was shrewd when it came to business, but he made a bad deal when he hooked up with that broad, as far as I'm concerned. Never had much time for me though. He was business, business, business."

On this particular evening, without another drink at hand, he ends his reminiscing early.

"Too bad you never met him. He was something. You're a lot like him. Real single-minded. Hardheaded, actually," he quips, flicking his finished Camel out of the window.

It strikes the abandoned house a few feet away and explodes into a thousand tiny embers. When I warn him that he is going to start a fire doing that, he observes that burning down that old rattrap would improve not only the neighborhood but our view as well.

His eyes begin to droop as he sits in the chair, but I am still wide awake, so I introduce a topic that is designed to resuscitate him.

"Were you married before?" I ask, knowing the answer, since my mother has mentioned another wife that he also treated poorly.

"None of your business. Why? Did your old lady say I was?"

No, I say, and change the subject. The facts of his prior life, the four decades before he married my mother, will remain mostly a mystery, even as I grill him for details in my adulthood. While he is all too willing to talk about his short-lived career as a radio crooner and his father's great prowess as a business mogul and his resentment for his Jean Harlow look-alike stepmother, he will reveal nothing about any prior marriages or personal relationships. This unwillingness to share the facts with me only raises my suspicions, and long after his death my sisters and I will speculate on whether we have half sisters or half brothers out there somewhere. My mother knows nothing concrete either, other than something he apparently let slip once about a former wife who was impossible to get along with, according to him. This is all she can say about it, except she figures he must have been pretty lousy to her too.

"Why are some men after you?" I ask. "The ones that came looking for you at Mom's," I add, further baiting the trap.

"What men?" he snaps, climbing from his languor. "What the hell are you talking about? Jesus, you got an imagination. Why would anybody be looking for me? Your mother is full of it from the word *go*."

"I think they were detectives with guns," I say, embellishing things.

"Shut up and go to bed. This is a dumb conversation. You're overtired and dreaming up things."

When I attempt to goad him further, he flips off the light and says that if I don't clamp it he will never take me to California. After our verbal jousting he sits chain-smoking in the dark while I attempt to score the final salvo by whistling "Rock around the Clock" over and over again for his benefit. It is a tune he truly detests.

Bitter Music

MY FAVORITE PARTS of the school day are lunch and geography, but making friends is not easy. A couple of weeks into the se-
mester I am approached in the schoolyard by a kid who says he
wants me to be his partner in music, or so I think.

"I choose you for Music," he says, and I say sure, not exactly certain what he means but willing to go along with it if it means gain-
ing a new friend.

When I readily accept his invitation he seems somewhat surprised. I follow him around the building, where a small crowd has
gathered.

"How come you picked on Music?" he asks accusingly, and I begin to get an idea of what is happening.

"Music?" I reply, still not clear what he means, and he points to a
kid in the crowd whom I remember bumping into in the hallway
that morning during the rush of the bell.

"That's Dondi Music. He says you pushed him. How come? Why
don't you pick on someone bigger? Like me. Come on—push me,
asshole."

A part of me wants to do just that, to knock him clear off his feet,
but I can't help imagining the possible grim consequences. He is
taller and broader than I am, maybe a seventh- or eighth-grader, and
his fists are clenched and ready for action. I know what Gary
Cooper or Alan Ladd would do, but the hero I am in my fantasies

resists translation to reality, so I ask to be left alone, swearing I will never bump into Music again. However, that is not good enough for Music's protector and defender, who knows he is about to score an easy victory.

"You chicken? Hey, everybody, he's chicken! Go ahead, I'll let you take the first punch," says Music's friend, holding his arms outstretched from his sides.

Someone in the crowd calls him Doyle and tells him to flatten the bag of bones, meaning me. I have been subjected to similar epithets before. When I reject his offer of first strike, he slaps me in the face. I feel stunned and humiliated, but my resolve to avoid all-out war with him is only deepened. Passivity is my defense. My way to stay alive. Few people shoot an unarmed man, I assure myself.

"Shit!" he shouts, clearly savoring his victory. "You're a friggin' baby. Hey, Music, you could take this little chickenshit yourself. Come on, take a punch, liver lips."

I remain inert in my resolve and shame as he administers yet another stinging blow to my cheek. The crowd of kids laughs and a couple of girls tell him to leave me alone as my eyes begin to mist over. There is no retaliation in me. I am a coward, yellow to the core, and I plan to vanish forever once my conqueror frees me.

"What are you, queer?" he asks, tauntingly pursing his lips and fluttering his eyelashes. "You use lipstick? How come your lips are so girly red, homo?"

He takes my lips between his fingers and pulls and pinches them. For a split second I am close to letting loose on him. Blasting his big beak with my fist. Kicking him in the stomach, and if he doesn't drop to the ground sobbing and pleading for mercy, running away as fast as my legs will carry me.

"You ever pick on my friend again, I'll beat the shit out of you. This was nothing, just a little spanking. You understand?"

Yes, I say, and he shakes his fist at me before marching triumphantly away, his entourage in tow. A kid, whom I figure to be Mexican because of his tan skin and coal-dark hair and eyes, remains behind, and I wonder if there is more trouble in store for me. He says something that I don't understand and then flips his finger at the receding crowd.

"Going to get my brother to kick his ass sometime. He try that on me, maybe I'll use this on him," he says, holding a sleek jackknife and snapping his wrist so that the long blade pops out. "Stiletto. You put some butter right here and it works real good. Comes out faster."

His name is Joey Ramone and he's three months younger than me, we determine. At his suggestion we play hooky the balance of the school day and go down by the railroad tracks where he claims he found a human thumb.

"Didn't have a nail on it either. Maybe it got cut off in a knife fight. Like this." He demonstrates, passing the bright blade of his knife across the knuckle of his thumb.

When it is almost dark we head in our separate directions. Joey has promised to recruit his big brother, Manny, to protect me too, and I no longer feel the need to disappear from the planet. Yet my cowardly behavior back at school leaves a bitter aftertaste in my mouth. I want another chance to show what I'm really made of but at the same time dread getting one.

On my way home I spot Doyle and his cronies and hide until they are long out of sight. If I make a stand it will be with Joey's brother at my side, or someone else able to keep me from being disfigured. The movies do not hire actors with scarred faces, I reason, unless it is for monster pictures. Back in our room I perforate the lid of a can of potatoes with a bottle opener, imagining it is Doyle's fat skull, and while I gulp down the bland contents of my supper I dream of reversing the events of the day, slashing at the air with my spoon.

Brussels Sprouts

FROM THE ROOF of our rooming house there is a clear view of the snowcapped Rocky Mountains. It has become my favorite place to pass the long, empty hours, although now that it is late October there is a chill to the wind that makes it uncomfortable at times. On these occasions I wrap myself like an Indian in the scratchy wool blanket from our bed.

My rocket radio works better on the roof than inside. I figure it has to do with the added height and the metal rod on the chimney to which I attach the set's alligator clip. A perfect antenna. Stations are loud and sharp except for the one I like the best, which features a deejay who howls like an animal and plays rock 'n' roll songs. He is called the Wolfman and sounds like no one I've ever heard. After several tries I think I have his wail down pretty well until the station fades and I am left with only the sound of my pathetic yelp. Late at night this station comes in better, and this is when I study the sky and do a lot of thinking.

If Ole Moses is right about the stars being the souls of the departed, then I am looking at Abraham Lincoln, Billy the Kid, and Humphrey Bogart. I wonder if Mr. Waller gets to eat all the Big Boy super cheeseburger deluxes he wants in heaven without getting fat. I wonder too if Squirt is back with his mother and if May is still walking around in her leopard-skin bikini. Some of the time I think about my sisters and more of the time about California and the whole new life that awaits me.

It has been three weeks since I watched TV with Web, so I descend to his first-floor apartment. He invites me in but has a peculiar look on his face.

"Mother's going to have to go to a nursing home. She's getting worse and they can take care of her better than I can."

I look over at her and see that she is smoking in her dreams again.

"The other day she couldn't breathe," Web continues, "and the oxygen tank blew a valve or seal . . . whatever you call it. It hissed like a deflating inner tube. She was turning blue. Thought she was going to die then and there, but she finally caught her breath and settled down. When she came around she asked for a Lucky."

Sugarfoot is on the television and there is an odd odor coming from the kitchen.

"You like brussels sprouts?" asks Web. "They're my favorite vegetable. I load them up with butter and salt. Taste great. Want some? They'll be done in a while. I cook them a long time because I hate them when they're hard."

As hungry as I am, I decline, not able to get beyond the unsavory smell that reminds me of loaded baby diapers. The western on TV is followed by a quiz show that gives away kitchen appliances. When we take our seats, Web asks if I have a girlfriend and I say not at the present time, adding that my former girlfriend's name was May. I tell him that she was very pretty and wore a bikini that let you see part of her behind, and he rubs his crotch and says that he sure could use a little pussy, a term that Joey Ramone from school uses all the time.

"Horny as hell. It's been a long time. Hard to do much with Mother to take care of all the time. Maybe I'll be able to get laid now that she's leaving. I can't really bring anybody here the way it looks and all," says Web, rubbing himself more vigorously. "You ever see a naked woman? Here, take a look at this one," he says as he pulls a magazine out from under the cushion of his reclining chair.

Holding the magazine open to a photo of a bare woman spread-eagled across a bale of hay, he says, "She's got a great ass, huh? How'd you like to slip your weenie between those cheeks?"

When he asks if it gives me a hard-on, I say it does, even though I'm only marginally familiar with the concept.

"Gives me one. Ever jerk off?" he asks, and I say once in a while, although this is another stretching of the truth.

A couple on the TV are jumping around and clutching at each other because they have won a self-defrosting Hotpoint refrigerator. When I turn back to Web, he has his penis in his hand and is slowly stroking it.

"I'll give you two dollars if you let me press against you. Don't worry—I won't do anything else, honest. Just come over here and sit against me. Please? You don't have to take your pants off or touch anything. Just a favor, Michael, okay? Here's two, no, make that three dollars."

Web removes the bills from his wallet while his diddle-dick protrudes from his fly, and I think about running from the apartment or punching my fist in his face, but instead I reluctantly move to his chair and take the money from him.

"Just turn around and push your butt on me for a minute," he instructs, guiding me as his breathing becomes louder and more erratic.

His jerking movements seem at once comical and strange to me and even though I know that what we're doing is not right, I don't think any real harm can come from it. Besides, if I don't play along I'll probably never be invited to watch television again, and then there is the money, I reason.

Suddenly he lets out a deep moan, quakes like a person being electrocuted, and then falls alarmingly still. His hands are pressed against his lap, and he looks like someone who has just dashed up ten flights of stairs.

"You better leave," he says after a long silence, and I ask why.

He is not feeling well, he says, still clutching his lap, which is covered with a milky fluid. "You can come back some other time. Don't say anything to your dad, okay? He wouldn't understand."

There are beads of perspiration on his forehead, and his flesh is the color of paste. Whatever has just occurred has made him woozy, I conclude, and I leave him slumped in his chair as all the quiz show contestants are brought back onstage to wave good-bye to the home audience. On my way out I am surprised to see that the old lady's eyes are wide open and fixed on the TV screen.

Little Flower

ON AN UNSEASONABLY warm day in early November I hang out with Joey and a new kid in our school named Eric Lumage, who has also had an encounter with the Doyle faction, although with less-humiliating results. He is nearly as skinny as me and at least an inch shorter, unlike Joey, who is my height but thickset. Joey says Eric and I look like a pair of stilts when we walk side by side, so we put him in the middle as we walk. He then remarks that we look like a bony guy with a big dong. When I inspect Eric's arms I am depressed to discover that his elbows are not as knobby as mine, and when Joey measures our wrists with his hand, I come up the loser.

"He's got almost half a finger more than you, Mike. You must be the thinnest kid in Denver, maybe the world," he announces matter-of-factly.

While it is in the seventies, the snow now extends well below the summits of the distant foothills, and most of the trees have been stripped of their leaves. They have been collected in tidy, colorful heaps in the sidewalk gutters of the well-groomed neighborhood we aimlessly wander through. Along the way we do our best to disturb the neat mounds, kicking leaves in every direction. This earns us dirty looks and unkind words from a few homeowners, and Joey is inspired to show us his improved technique for flipping the blade of his stiletto after one particularly vehement tongue-lashing by a local resident.

"Maybe I'm the fastest in the West," he boasts, snapping his wrist with lightning speed that causes the shiny steel blade to eject instantaneously.

He allows us to practice our own technique with his knife, but we don't come close to matching his skill.

"Gringos don't know how to do it," he observes with an air of superiority as he springs the lance from its onyx casing. "You guys could get killed by the time you get it open. Guts be on the ground for the maggots to eat."

We desperately want stilettos of our own but can't afford them, so Joey suggests that we cop some from a pawnshop downtown.

Easy as pussy," says Joey, waving his treasure under our noses. "We go in and one of us asks to see something, like those fancy guitars they got, and while the guy is showing them, one of us reaches over the counter and grabs the knives. I been in there with my brother and it would be nothing."

The next day we plan to go down and check out the place. "Case it," says Joey, who knows a lot of terms related to robbing stores. Eric says he'll do the clipping. He claims he's done stuff like that before, but Joey says he's full of it.

"Yeah, back in Ohio I stole a Timex lady's watch from a drugstore for my grandmother's birthday, and I didn't have any help either," he swears, with a smug expression on his little boy's face.

Up ahead there is a kid about our age, maybe twelve or thirteen, delivering newspapers from a sack wrapped around the handlebars of his bicycle. Eric asks for Joey's knife and says he's going to rob the paperboy.

"Come on, you ain't gonna do nothing," responds Joey, who hands Eric the knife as if to challenge him.

With the weapon in hand Eric jogs in the direction of the paperboy, who is about a block away.

"He's just putting on a show," remarks Joey. "Probably gonna ask for a free paper or something."

We hold our ground and watch as Eric converses with the

paperboy and then to our enormous surprise flips the knife open. The paperboy hands something to him and speeds away on his bike. We are amused by the scene and genuinely impressed when Eric returns with a haul of $2.50.

"What'd he say when he saw the stiletto open?" inquires Joey, grinning broadly.

" 'Please don't hurt me,' " replies Eric in a falsetto voice.

We all laugh at that and then discuss how best to spend the bounty. Joey suggests we get something to chow on at the grocery store up ahead. This especially appeals to me because I've been running on a stale donut all day. With the loot divided three ways we load up on candy, chips, and soda and pool what we have left for some bread and salami.

We quickly settle on a spot to partake of our feast, but before we can swallow our first bite a police car appears.

"Cops!" shouts Eric, and we drop our food and run.

At the corner there is another cruiser, so we shift direction and cut through a yard in order to reach the next street over. None of this seems real to me. I feel like an actor in a television melodrama, but this time I'm the bad guy.

We are outmaneuvered. The police are waiting for us when we emerge from a driveway, but Joey has already spotted them and disappeared over a fence, leaving me and Eric trapped. The policemen tell us to freeze and put our hands up and they search our clothing.

"Where's the knife you used to stick up the paperboy?" one of them asks us, and Eric plays dumb.

"What paperboy?" he replies, and this earns him a slap in the face.

Tears roll from Eric's eyes and I figure I'm next. Another police car approaches and I spot Joey seated in the back. Then the paperboy arrives with his father, and a policeman asks if we're the ones who took his money. The paperboy says we are, pointing a finger at Eric. With that we are hauled away to the juvenile detention center to be booked.

"You little punks know that you committed armed robbery?" asks the officer who struck Eric. "That's a felony. Might spend a little time in juvy hall for this one. Maybe even end up in Golden. You know what they do with runts like you up there?"

Without offering an answer, he turns to his partner and snickers. In a few minutes we are escorted into a brick building that I notice has no bars on its window as I expect. This both relieves and disappoints me. Not a real jail, I think. Inside we are asked to remove everything from our pockets and place it into a brown envelope and to take a seat in a room where talking is prohibited. One by one we are interrogated about the robbery. When it is my turn I decide to explain everything just as it happened, which requires squealing on Eric. But it really wasn't my fault or Joey's, I reason, so why should we go to the slammer? Still I feel a little like a traitor when I recount the unfortunate event to a man in a short crew cut and black horn-rim glasses seated behind a gray metal desk. He isn't anything like the police who arrested us. In fact he is very soft spoken and friendly.

"Tell me, Michael, who robbed the paperboy?" he asks, and I give him all the bleak details, particularly stressing Eric's role and my lack of involvement.

"So you and the other kid, Joey, didn't tell your friend to do it?"

No, I say, and explain that we thought he was only kidding when he said he was going to do it.

"But he told you he was going to rob the paperboy, and that makes you and your friend accessories," he says, explaining what the word means and how that makes us as guilty as Eric.

"You could be sent to the Golden Juvenile Detention Facility for this," he says, and I remember the policeman's remark.

Despite every effort, I cannot contain my tears. I don't want to end up in prison and have a criminal record as this man says may happen. This is not what I had in mind for my future. An actor or maybe a veterinarian, but not an ex-con. At any moment I half expect the man to say that he hopes I have learned my lesson and that I can go, but deep down I know that isn't going to happen. Maybe my whole life is ruined, I think, fighting back the encroaching sobs.

"Look, I want you to write down on this piece of paper everything you just told me, okay? What you kids did wasn't very smart, but maybe you'll get off a little easier than the one with the knife," says the juvenile official, measuring my reaction.

Later I am locked in a small cubicle, or cell, with a younger boy, who won't reveal why he too is incarcerated. Despite his silence on the subject, I talk about my crime and for his ears only I embellish my part in the heist. In my significantly altered account I am the one with the stiletto, and I confide in him that I've held up a few other people as well but never been caught before. Foremost in his mind is the fear of being sent to Golden, and as soon as I hear the word I recant my story and confess that this is my first offense as well, adding that it wasn't even my doing.

"The big kids beat you up. Some are even murderers. Do you think they'll send us there?" he asks, his words filled with trepidation, and I say that they might, although I can't believe that will actually happen to me.

This makes him tremble and he wraps himself in his blanket. I feel in command and propose that if he'll let me hypnotize him, I can give him powers against those who would hurt him. At the start he is reluctant to play along, but when I tell him that they use stilettos on new kids in Golden he goes along with my idea.

Employing Count Dracula's technique in the movies, I stare deeply into his eyes and tell him he is getting very sleepy. My cell mate obligingly closes his eyes and I concoct a speech that borrows from what Ole Moses said about the stars and a story I read in a comic book.

"Whenever anybody wants to beat you up or stab you with a stiletto, call on Zuma Nova, the Prince Beast of the Dark Planet. He will protect you and give you the powers of the great sky spirits. All you have to say is . . ." And here I pause to come up with something really impressive, which turns out to be a mysterious term I recall being used by an old Italian man who lived on an upper floor in my mother's building back in Albany. "Pastafagooli," I proclaim, and I repeat the word a second time with added dramatic flare.

In his convincing trance my subject repeats the mystical word along with me until there is a bang on the door and a voice telling us to shut up. After a few seconds I ask my fellow inmate how he feels, and he whispers that he is much better, not scared anymore, although he looks at me like I am a little crazy.

"Pastafagooli," he says with a tentative smile on his freckled face as he pulls the blanket over his head.

That night I pray to the Little Flower of Jesus to get me out of this terrible predicament. According to family legend, a devotional card depicting the Little Flower of Jesus was placed under my sick aunt's pillow the night she lay dying from pneumonia, and in the morning she was sitting up in her bed and taking nourishment— cinnamon toast and tea, as the story goes.

She was only five years old at the time, and my mother's family considered her amazing recovery a bona fide miracle. "Always pray to the Little Flower when you need help" was my mother's advice to me and my sisters from as far back as I can remember.

I doubt if the Little Flower of Jesus listens to criminals, I think, but I give it a shot just in case.

Phrenologist's Dream

RECLINING ON MY BUNK with my hand resting on the back of my head, I am reminded of how misshapen my skull is and this deepens my feeling of self-pity. It's a sad and embarrassing fact to me that my noggin is very flat on one side, resulting in two very different profiles, neither of which is very attractive because of the bump on the bridge of my nose.

"It's a Roman nose," my father often says to needle me when I complain about it. "It roams all over your face."

"Yours is so big it roams all over the globe," is my standard comeback.

When I bring up the irregular shape of my head, he always asserts that my mother is to blame because she never rotated me when I was in my crib. That was her job and not his, he counters, when I ask why he didn't move me around either.

"Mothers are responsible for that sort of thing," he tells me. "I wasn't around because I was trying to make a living. Your old lady couldn't even get that right, so you can thank her for your head being that way, not me."

The more I think about this the angrier I get. Some parents I have, I fume, as I measure my deformity time and again in the mirror. Stupid dopes! They couldn't even make sure their child's head would be round like everyone else's.

I worry that I might have less brain matter than people with normally shaped heads because one side is so indented compared to the other side and this would probably reduce the space my brain has to grow in. My apprehension intensifies when I think that someday my head might just pop open from the pressure of my brain pushing against the interior walls of my skull or that I might remain stuck with the underdeveloped brain of a twelve-year-old as my body grows into adulthood. Maybe too I might become crazy because the part of the brain that makes a person sane may be located where my head is compressed.

All in all, this is another mark against my future prospects, I conclude, and maybe being here in jail is the first sign that something is starting to go terribly wrong with me. Words cannot express how relieved I am when sleep overtakes me. Not even Zuma Nova, the Prince Beast of the Dark Planet, can combat my demons as mightily as the sandman when he is in peak form, and this night he is, since the bad dreams are kept at bay.

Golden Moments

MY FATHER SAYS I have been assigned a lawyer and should be out of this place soon. At first I think he is joking.

"A lawyer?" I ask incredulously, images of Perry Mason filling my head.

"Yeah, what you and your stupid buddies did was a crime, whether you know it or not," he answers.

I'm still not sure I believe him, because there is liquor on his breath and the telltale watery look in his eyes.

"Maybe they're going to send you kids to the big house. Sing Sing, maybe," he quips while attempting to steady the match in his hand.

He sees that his remark has a disturbing effect on me and tries to lift my spirits by promising to leave Denver as soon as this ordeal is over.

"They say you and that Mexican kid didn't really do anything but watch. You were just there, so you should get off easy. They have to set a court date, and the lawyer says they should release you until then. Just no more armed robberies when you get out, Machine Gun Kelly," he says, trying to conceal his amusement with my discomfort.

The idea of going to court sets off an alarm in me. Courts are places where prison sentences are handed out, I think.

"The father of the boy you jerks robbed won't drop the charges and is mad as a son of a bitch. Wants you all to go to the pokey. Says the knife was big as hell. A bayonet or something."

A stiletto, I tell him, and reiterate the fact that I didn't actually do the robbing.

"Yeah, but you were quick enough to help spend the loot, weren't you?" he says, and then proceeds to criticize me for making friends with Joey, or that spick kid, as he calls him. "All those wetbacks are hoodlums. They're good for nothing but committing crimes. You better be more selective in choosing your friends in the future, or you're always going to be in this kind of trouble."

There are several other inmates and their parents in the visiting area, but I don't see either Joey or Eric.

"When can I leave?" I ask, and my father, who is still turning the screw, says in a month or two.

When I balk at this, he smirks and adjusts his estimate downward to a day or so. The visiting hour ends, and I am herded away with my fellow inmates to my cell and told to gather up my things because I am being transferred to a different one. I'm informed that my cell mate has been shipped off to Golden.

"You can't get away with what he did and go walking free," says the guard who escorts me to my new quarters.

When I ask what it was he did that was so awful, recalling his meek manner, I'm told to mind my own business and that I better hope I don't end up the same way.

"You stab someone and you're gonna do some hard time. That boy had a real bad streak, and he won't see the light of day until he's twenty-one," concedes my chaperone, and when I ask who the stabbing victim was he repeats his previous statement about minding my own business.

There are two older boys and four beds in the room that I'm taken to. One of the boys reminds me of Music's guardian. He's large and unfriendly-looking. I feel abandoned in a potential lion's den when the door is closed and locked behind me. When I sit on one of the empty beds, I'm told that it is already taken, so I move to another.

"That one's taken too," says Doyle's twin, whose T-shirt sleeves are pulled up over his brawny shoulders.

"'Fraid you have to sack out on the floor," he says, but I don't move and this wins me hostile looks from both of them.

During the evening meal I see Eric and Joey, but we have all been assigned to sit at different tables. Joey smiles and nods, but Eric avoids looking at either one of us. The food is the best I have had since Pearl's back in Indiana. The mashed potatoes are especially sumptuous, but my appetite is off because of my dread about returning to my cell.

Not long after we return and are locked in for the night, the Doyle look-alike begins to taunt me, saying that I'm as ugly as a hairy turd. He approaches my bed, followed by his accomplice, and pokes my chest with his index finger.

"That hurt, puke head? No? Well, does this?" he asks, poking me harder. "I'm gonna make you give me a blow job," he says, placing his hand over his fly and moving to within a couple of inches of my face.

His cohort laughs and says he should wait until after the lights go out. My head is spinning and I feel panicked. I don't know what to do. If I call for the guard, what can I tell him that will get me out of this cell? I wonder, and if he is unsympathetic, calling him could make things even worse for me.

When the lights are turned off I brace myself for what is to come. Both boys begin making threatening statements and noises but after a while they become silent. A long time passes as I await my fate, but the sound of snoring puts me at ease enough to fall asleep myself. When the morning wake-up bell rings I am relieved to find that I am still in one piece. Both of my cell mates are slow to rise and not the least bit interested in my existence now.

Following breakfast I return to my cell and find Doyle's look-alike packing his belongings into a duffel bag. The other boy remarks that they are sending him to Golden, and when he says this there is a loud sniffle from his friend, who is no longer the monster of the day before. His expression has been altered by remorse and anxiety.

"I don't want to go," he mumbles when the door opens and the guard enters to take him away.

"Ready for your little ride?" asks the guard, clearly enjoying what I deduce is a familiar and pleasing ritual for him. "Maybe you little angels will be next to go up to the Big G," he says, leading his charge out of the cell.

That afternoon I am turned over to the custody of my father, who takes me back to our rooming house and naps until it is time for his shift at the hotel. There are a handful of eggs and a few slices of stale bread on the table next to the glass of water containing his upper plate. I boil an egg in a badly dented metal pan whose handle is about to fall off until the egg is semihard, the way I like it, and then carefully spread it over a slice of the bread. As I gulp it down, my father says to go easy on the grub because he can't buy more until the day after tomorrow.

Half asleep, he informs me that my court date is in three days and that he still hasn't been able to scrounge up enough dough to get us a bus ticket. Maybe by the end of the month, he says.

"What if I go to jail?" I ask as he pulls the covers up around his unshaven chin, and he replies that I worry too much.

"You won't go to jail, for God sake. Just like your old lady. Always got to think the worst is gonna happen," he mutters through the discolored end of the bedspread.

Once he's sleeping I contemplate running away. I'll go to California on my own, I think, but instead I end up on the roof trying to distinguish the buildings that might belong to the Golden Juvenile Detention Facility from those of the Coors Brewing Company, all of which rest against the bleak, snowy hills some twenty miles in the distance.

Probation and Revelation

MY COURT DATE has arrived and my father is dry. He hasn't had a drink in several days and it looks like this may be the start of a stretch of sobriety for him. While I'm hopeful about this, I'm afraid that my case may be heard by what my father calls a hostile judge. Needling me, he says I'll probably draw Denver's infamous hanging judge. My court-appointed lawyer says we should all get off with a warning and some probation. It helps that none of us has a previous record, he says. Not even the Mexican kid? asks my father.

Nonetheless, in the judge's austere chambers my stomach tightens and I fear the worst is about to happen. The judge's expression is solemn and I can tell that even my father is nervous.

"You lads know what you did was extremely wrong. In the eyes of the law it is called a felony. Armed robbery is a despicable act and one that must be dealt with in a fitting manner."

Upon hearing these stern words, Eric begins to sniffle and I am on the verge of joining him. Joey shows little emotion as he sits next to his mother, who is outfitted in black from head to toe as if she were in mourning. There is a deep scar beneath her left eye, and a single tear flows along its groove and hangs at the end of it like an icicle in a trough. Rosary beads snake through the fingers of her clenched right hand and she unconsciously taps the crucifix against the wooden leg of her chair. Its steady rhythmic cadence closely matches the judge's spoken words, I notice.

"However," he continues, "given the fact"—clack-clack—"that this is a first"—clack-clack—"offense for each of you"—clack-clack—"and that you are all"—clack-clack—"appropriately contrite . . ."

Here he pauses and asks us if that is indeed the case, and without any idea of what the word means, we all know enough to answer in the affirmative.

"Good," he says, looking each of us in the eyes. "Therefore I am inclined to forgo a sentence involving incarceration in the fervent hope that you have learned a lesson from this unfortunate experience and will never break the law again. If any of you do, be assured you will be sentenced to the juvenile detention facility for a lengthy stay. I do, however, sentence all three of you to one year's probation. If during this period you get into any trouble at all, I will hear about it and take appropriate action. Do you understand?"

Everybody in the room, including the adults, says yes, and the judge dismisses us. Twice a month I am to report to my probation officer. If I miss an appointment I am in violation of the judge's order and this, I am reminded, could result in "time." When I remark to my father that Eric got off as easy as we did, he says not quite, that he must report to his probation officer weekly. Big deal, I complain, and my father says the judge probably took into consideration that Eric was a year younger than us. This information surprises me because he claimed to be going on twelve too.

On our way back to the rooming house my father warns me against getting into any more trouble, and I counter by saying that I wouldn't have gotten into this mess in the first place if we were in California. This rubs him the wrong way and he expresses his irritation by kicking what appears to be an empty milk carton resting on the edge of the sidewalk. To his shock and dismay, what remains of its contents ends up on his shoes and pant leg. Bristling, he dabs at the splatter with a clump of toilet paper that he always keeps in his back pocket. I don't dare laugh because his anger is way past the boiling point.

"You can get into trouble anyplace, you little jerk, if you're that kind of person. Just stay the hell away from those little crumb-bums, especially that wetback. He's trouble. You can see it written all over him. Real bad news, that one. Shit, this is going to leave a stain!"

My protests do little to alter his opinion of my friends, so in retaliation I dig into my bag of insults, finding something that is certain to goad him further. What I come up with is a snide remark about his habit of picking his ample beak, which he is doing at the moment with considerable vigor, having returned the shredded tissue to his pocket.

"Digging for gold?" I ask, and he tells me to shut my damn trap before he gives me a good crack in the ass. "I already have a crack in my ass and if you keep picking your nose like that your hand's going to come out in China," I continue, throwing caution to the wind but keeping a safe distance from him in case he decides to act on his threat.

What really gets to me about his nose picking is that he usually wipes his boogers onto the crepe soles of his worn-out Hush Puppies. That makes my stomach contract, and when I suggest that he use his tissue like everyone else, he says he'd rather have snot on the bottom of his shoe than in his pocket.

I remark that my mother also hated it when he dug at his nose, and he replies that she hated everything he did and then some. We spend the balance of our walk home in silence. On our way up to our room we bump into Web, who asks how things went at the courthouse. My father remarks that I haven't been sent to Alcatraz yet.

"*Have Gun's* on tonight," he shouts up after us.

Although I have little intention of taking him up on his offer, I yell back that I'll be down later.

"Stay out of there," orders my father as if he is on to Web.

After he has gone to work I gather all our old magazines and comics together with the idea of trading them for different ones at the used-book store a couple of blocks over on Colfax. Instead I swap the lot for a dog-eared copy of *Robinson Crusoe,* which captures my interest after I read the first page. I'm also intrigued by the notion of actually reading an entire book, something I have never done.

Back in our room I lose myself in this remarkable tale of survival and perseverance, and another world is suddenly opened up to me, one that provides me escape from the tedium and loneliness that are such an integral part of my daily existence.

'Tis the Season

I RETURN TO THE used-book store several times over the next weeks. Among other books I like are *Winnie-the-Pooh* and *Charlotte's Web,* whose title I can't help but connecting with our landlord. On Thanksgiving I reread *Robinson Crusoe* while my father prepares a meal of fried calf's liver, the best kind of liver, he claims, and canned yams before he goes off to work.

"Place will be dead, but it's time and a half," he says, attempting to pry open the can of yams with the bottle opener—*church key* is his term for it. Only partially succeeding, he is forced to dig out the orange contents with a fork. In the middle of doing this, the can and its syrupy contents go flying. He is about to boot the container across the room when I scoop it up and salvage what's left. We end up with a kind of yam mush that tastes a lot better than it looks.

"Dinner is served," I proclaim in the lavishly formal style of a British butler I recall seeing in a movie about rich people, and this breaks me up, considering our scant repast.

Christmas dinner is less lavish. Scrambled eggs and leftover fried SPAM slices, which resemble little pieces of soap before they're re-fried, constitute the menu, and again my father is scheduled to run the elevator at the Hotel Ames. There are no presents under the tree because there is no tree. The day is like any other, aside from my deep sense that I am being deprived of something that the rest of the world is enjoying.

I wonder how my mother and sisters are doing and when I suggest that we get in touch with them, even a collect call, my father rejects the idea outright. She'll go crazy, he says, adding that he doesn't need any more grief than he already has, nor cops on his tail.

"Do you think they're after us?" I ask, as much to rile him as to get his view on a subject that has entered my thoughts more than a few times.

"That's ridiculous," he snaps, but his expression betrays his words.

In the evening, when I listen to Christmas carols on my rocket radio, loneliness comes crashing down on me harder than ever before, and I decide to visit Web. Any company is better than none. It is several moments before he answers my knocks, and when he does he says he has been visiting his mother in the nursing home for Christmas and it has drained him. He is going right to bed, he says, and practically slams the door in my face. I return to my room feeling like the last person on earth.

Later up on the roof my spirits are momentarily lifted by the sight of snow falling in thick sheets. Out on the dark prairie I imagine a cowboy sitting alone by his campfire as the snow accumulates on the brim of his hat. I mix my own music for this vision by whistling a medley of my favorite western theme songs.

As the snow gathers on the blanket I'm wrapped in, I also fantasize rescuing Claudia and Pamela from a giant avalanche. My act of bravery makes the headlines all over the world and catches the attention of President Eisenhower, who awards me a medal for my courage.

"Merry Christmas," says his kindly wife, Mamie, and the vast audience assembled at the White House beams at me as my favorite carol, as performed by the Chipmunks, is played.

High Noon

JOEY, ERIC, AND I are prohibited from playing together, and my probation officer, Mr. Chicorski (who I doubt knows what I look like because he never lifts his pale face up from his cluttered desk when he speaks to me) says that if we're caught doing so, we'll be in serious trouble. "Got that?" he says twice in a row, and when I attempt to answer he tells me not to speak while he's talking.

"You're here to listen this time. In the future I'll have specific questions for which I will expect very direct answers. This is not a coffee klatch, mister. I have a lot of you boys to deal with, so the less said the better. Got that? Good," he says, when I don't answer, and then he tells me to take off.

Eric is absent from school a few days before I learn that he has been returned to live with his grandparents in Ohio. Somehow Joey's brother, Manny, has learned that Eric's father beat up his wife and put her in the hospital. Apparently when coming to her defense, Eric got punched in the face and ended up with a couple of broken teeth, so they sent him away, reports Joey.

"This would take care of that motherfucker," he says, showing me his new stiletto. We are spotted talking to one another in the hall by the principal, Mr. Black, and we pretend we're just passing each other in the hope we won't be reported. This is the first time I have spoken with Joey since court, and we make tentative plans to meet down by the railroad tracks the next day.

A kid named Ronny Bartlett, whose homeroom desk is directly

behind mine, has been needling and harassing me. He shoots rubber bands and flicks objects at my back, referring to me as a flathead bony freak. Once he even spits at me, but I'm afraid to confront him because he is at least a foot taller than I am.

When he leans over and whispers that he's going to get me after class like Doyle did, I know I have to do something to avoid another humiliating scene. In the final moments before the lunch bell rings, I think of something James Cagney once said in a gangster movie, about getting your enemy before he gets you, and I devise a plan based on this maxim.

As we are filing out of class, Bartlett challenges me to a fight after school, and I say, "Why wait?" and tell him that we should go at it right now. This show of bravado catches him off guard but he agrees to my proposal. I carefully gauge his exact position as he stands in front of me, and then I slowly turn my back to him and hand my book to a kid standing in the crowd that has formed. At the precise instant the book leaves my hands, I reel around and catch my foe squarely on his nose with my fist. He is shocked and stunned and as he gropes for his face he topples backward onto the floor, blood pouring from his nostrils. The kids witnessing this are as astonished by my surprise assault as he is. I catch sight of Doyle in the crowd, and he too has a look of awe on his face. Although I'm feeling a little shaken by my actions, a sense of satisfaction overtakes me. Zuma Nova has arrived, I want to yell out. Bullies beware! I shout triumphantly to myself.

Someone has summoned my homeroom teacher, Mrs Appleton, and by the time she reaches the scene there is a pool of blood on the floor where Bartlett is kneeling. She demands to know who did this and when I step forward she looks at me like I must be joking. We are escorted to the principal's office, where first aid is administered to Bartlett's crumpled nose. Ice cubes wrapped in a towel do little to slow the bleeding, and my pleasure gives way to concern. The principal tells us that his nose is probably broken and then he looks at me as if to ask how someone so puny can cause so much damage.

We're both suspended and told not to return to school until

Monday. This doesn't seem like harsh punishment to me, considering that it is Thursday.

"That's a week from this Monday," he clarifies, and the situation seems graver all of a sudden.

I have no telephone, so Mr. Black writes a note for me to deliver to my father, warning that if he doesn't respond to him about this unfortunate incident I'll be in even more hot water.

When I report to my father what has happened, he is more interested in how I managed to deck a kid so much bigger than me than he is in the suspension and request from the principal to see him next week.

"If they report this to Chicorski, your little goose is cooked, Jack Dempsey," he says, running things over in his head.

This has occurred to me too and now it hits me that this fight could be enough to get me sent to Golden, even if it wasn't my fault.

"Nothing's ever your fault, for Christ's sake," he snaps at me.

"There was nothing I could do. He was going to kill me after school like Doyle," I say defensively, and he asks who the hell Doyle is.

Because of my embarrassment I have not told him about that encounter, so I quickly redirect the conversation back to Bartlett, who I say is always beating up smaller kids.

"Well, there's nothing wrong in sticking up for yourself," he says, adding that it might not be so easy to convince the judge again that I wasn't the instigator.

The next morning we bundle up as best we can in coats we've gotten from a thrift shop on Colfax Avenue. His is a tired beige raincoat with a temperamental zip-in lining, and mine is a moth-eaten wool job with two buttons missing. We then go to the Hotel Ames so that he can pick up his check, which we learn at the bus station will take us to Laramie, Wyoming. It is time to leave our problems behind, says my father, and that is splendid with me. From there we'll hitch a ride west to Salt Lake City and then southwest to Los Angeles. That is our plan anyway.

At long last our trip to California is resumed, during what my father complains is the worst time of year to be bumming a ride across the Rockies. Before we reach the Denver city limits, his forebodings are validated by a sudden snow squall so intense that our bus driver comments that we'll be lucky to get through it. While I find the whole thing exciting, my father acts like he is awaiting the fall of the guillotine's blade.

"Great . . . just great," he mumbles, staring at the white abyss beyond the bus window.

PART IV
DENVER TO LOS ANGELES
(1,023 Miles)

Road to Saint George

IT IS EARLY MORNING when we reach Laramie. The ride has taken three times longer than scheduled because of the storm, which has mercifully moved east to the Nebraska Panhandle, reports the bus driver. Bright sunshine is left in its wake, vastly improving my father's view of the world. We can breathe easy, he says in a sudden burst of optimism, his cares momentarily vanishing as they usually do when he lights a fresh cigarette.

We stand on the two-lane highway at the western outskirts of town and are pummeled by winds that roar down on us from the frozen peaks of the Laramie Mountains. The icy battering, intensified by quickly passing cars and trucks, causes my nose to run incessantly. If I don't scrape under it frequently, the snot forms into a hard crust and when I move my upper lip it feels like a scab breaking apart.

Meanwhile my father is battling with his flapping hair and about to call it quits when a car with a Utah plate stops and turns our mounting despair into joy. This is a ride of substance, I expect, and in fact it turns out that the driver is going to Saint George, a town in the southwestern corner of the Beehive State, as the Rand McNally I have all but memorized calls it. My father says it is home to a bunch of religious nuts called Mormons, who have many wives and hundreds of kids. He says he doesn't mind the several wives part, but forget all the kids, especially if they're a pain in the ass like me, he teases. I calculate that this is a lift of more than seven hundred miles and I'm ecstatic to say the least.

At the end of this jump we'll be one state away from California, and not really a whole state either. Only the pointy lower part of Nevada will stand between us and the Golden State, a nickname that has lost some of its charm since my scrape with the law in the Mile High City.

The driver is a small bald guy with a high-pitched voice, who introduces himself as Foster. He goes by his last name, he says, because he can't stand his first, which he doesn't divulge. Herbert or Cecil are names that I think suit him. He is an appraiser for an insurance company and his home is Ogden. He says he's been in Cheyenne on business and is going straight on down to Saint George for the same reason, and we're welcome to ride along if we like. We like.

"Little fire at a filling station back there," he reports. "Lucky it didn't blow to smithereens. I'm heading to Saint George to look at foundation damage to an office building. Government's been testing bombs, big ones, around that area for years. Could be a contributing factor, although you'd be hard pressed to prove it. My guess is that's what's causing the trouble. Anyway, I get a chance to visit my little brother who lives there. He's got cancer and he's just thirty-four. Imagine that. Has a couple of kids, both boys, and a real sweet wife, Lilly."

While my father and Foster enthusiastically discuss fires—a topic my father has always enjoyed—and a multitude of other issues, I drink in the western scenery and follow our progress with our tattered map as we pass through the Medicine Bow Mountains heading toward Rawlins and cross the Continental Divide, which cuts just in front of Rock Springs. Road signs denote distinctly western places: FLAMING GORGE, BITTER CREEK, FORT BRIDGER, RELIANCE. I wonder what it would be like to live in such exotic locations, to ride the open range between jagged snowcapped peaks on a horse as fast and beautiful as Flicka.

The conversation in the front seat turns to World War II. Foster

served in the South Pacific and received a medal. My father recounts the war mishap that led to his back injury and slightly at-
tenuated index finger but no commendation. According to this
version of the story there is a fatality involved.

"We flipped over on some ice up in the Aleutians. My buddy
didn't make it, and I hurt my lower spine and this finger pretty
good. That got me back stateside with an honorable discharge."

"You didn't get the Purple Heart?" asks Foster, and my father
complains that he did not but adds that he is looking into it.

"Why, hell yes. I would," agrees Foster.

Another account of how his finger got its stumpy appearance involves his getting it caught in bicycle spokes when he was a kid. I'm
not sure which story to believe. I like the one about the war but am
inclined to go with the bike account. On the numerous occasions
when we argue, I claim that his finger got its stubby appearance
from his using it to pick his nose all the time.

"Went to work for Pratt and Whitney in Hartford until the war
ended. My back still flares up and this finger only bends so far," says
my father, demonstrating his finger's lack of flexibility.

We reach Salt Lake City a few hours after sunset and are put up
for the night in a small motel, compliments of our driver, who my
father practically elevates to sainthood for his act of generosity. Not
long after daybreak we're back on the road. The landscape reminds
me of movies with cavemen and prehistoric animals, and when I
make this observation Foster says that what we're passing is nothing compared to the country around a place called Moab, east of
where we are.

"You think you're back in Paleolithic times when you get a gan-
der of the stone arches and cliffs over there. Take a raft down the
Colorado through Glen Canyon and you think you're back millions
of years. Great place to camp too."

My father comments that while it's interesting country all right
he prefers places with a few more humans. Towns with evocative
names like Thistle, Nephi, Manti, and Paragonah possess no appeal

to him, whereas they represent the very stuff of my dreams and fantasies.

"Kind of a godforsaken place. I mean there's not much out here, is there? No decent-size cities or hotels, that is," he notes while nervously scanning the sparse horizon.

This launches him into a discussion about the hotel business and a lengthy description of the big eastern hotels he's worked at. Foster says that just last month he had to estimate the damages caused by someone smoking in bed at a hotel near Jackson Hole, Wyoming.

"The lodge has about twenty-five rooms, I'd guess, maybe a few more. Real nice ones too. TV and all. Could have burned to the ground. It used to be a house of ill repute around the turn of the century, or so legend has it. Supposedly Teddy Roosevelt and other famous folks stayed there in its glory days. Red velour furniture, bear rugs all over the floors, and moose heads on the walls. Pretty swank. My wife and I spent our second honeymoon there a few years back, so for sentimental reasons I was glad it didn't burn down."

Around two in the afternoon we're dropped off on a highway just west of the center of Saint George and wished good luck by Foster, who reaches into his pocket and hands my father a five-dollar bill.

"God bless you," responds my father, and his remark seems out of character and funny to me although I'm thrilled by our benefactor's kind deed.

"God bless you," I mimic when the car pulls away, and my father ignores my taunt while happily pocketing his newfound fortune. Although it is sunny, the air is frigid and my father's resolve to catch another ride quickly deteriorates.

"We'll try this awhile and then head into town before we freeze to death. We can get a room for the night and hit the road bright and early in the morning," he says, and this time I'm not at odds with his plan because I am chilled to the bone and my nose is beginning to drain and ice up again. On top of all that, my everlasting constipation is acting up and causing me occasional sharp abdominal pains. When I reveal this to my father, he recommends bouncing up and down on the balls of my feet to ease my cramps and loosen my severely clogged bowels. His prescription relieves my stomachache but I'm convinced that I'll never be able to go to the bathroom on a daily basis like normal people.

Just as we agree to give it ten more minutes, a car with California plates responds to our pleading thumbs. "Yahoo!" I shout at the top of my lungs as we jog to the car, and my father tells me to shush up. He doesn't want the driver to think we're crazy and drive away.

California . . . Los Angeles . . . Encino!

I THINK I'M HAPPIER than I have been in my whole life. I can hardly believe it. We have actually made it, but not without walking until the bottoms of my feet are burning and my father is complaining that his back is flaring up. During the past day my big toe has worn a small hole in the top of one of my canvas shoes. This, however, is of minor concern to me because we are now in the land of palm trees and movie stars. I imagine every person we see is connected in some way to Republic or Allied Pictures.

When at long last we catch sight of the Encino Paradise Motel as we trudge down Sepulveda Boulevard, we slip into the rest room of a gas station to remove some of the grime from our travel in preparation for greeting my father's friend, who works at the motel and has told my father there may be a job for him as well.

A pool surrounded by a chain-link fence is located in front of the motel. Despite its being winter the temperature feels warm enough to use it, yet there are no swimmers in sight. A miniature golf course runs from the pool area to the parking lot next to the motel's office. The entire complex is painted pastel green and there are pink flamingos stenciled on all the doors.

"Nice place," remarks my father, and I fully agree.

"Are we going to stay here?" I ask, and he says he sure hopes so, citing the fact that his pal does.

A heavyset man in a short-sleeved knit shirt covered with tiny

fishing poles and feathered hooks greets us as we enter. His arms in-
trigue me because they are blanketed in black hair that conceals any
hint of flesh. The same is true of the area around the collar of his
shirt, where long strands of hair stick out like furry tarantula legs.
This is the hairiest person I have ever seen . . . a gorilla in human
clothing. He asks if we'd like a room, and my father tells him that
we're looking for Frank Belrose.

"Not here anymore. Why?" he asks in a less friendly tone, and my
father says that he is a friend from his hotel days.

"Well, your friend hit the sauce, so I had to let him go. Damn
nuisance. Bothered my guests, especially the women, and did shitty
work too. Good riddance, I say. So what kind of hotel work do you
do?"

"Mostly bellhop and handle the door," responds my father with
a mix of disappointment and hope in his voice.

"We don't have bellhops and doormen in the motel business, at
least not at this one, but if you can manage a paintbrush you're welcome to finish what your buddy started."

My father says he's done tons of painting in his day and would
appreciate the job, especially since he has to meet my basic needs, et
cetera, et cetera. The matter of wages is settled and to my delight we
are taken to what will be our residence during his employment at
the motel.

"Put you in number seventeen, where your friend was. Left it a
mess, the moron. Booze bottles and crap all over the place. Bitch to
clean up. It has a hot plate and a small refrigerator, but we don't allow any heavy cooking. Light stuff. You know, canned soup and
things like that."

I take the room number to be a magical sign because the seven-
teenth is the date of my birthday. The idea of staying in a southern
California motel with a pool and a miniature golf course is as-
tounding to me and when I find that our room has a TV I am
nearly delirious. This is beyond anything I expected or dreamed of.

That night we clip a can of sardines in tomato sauce from a

neighborhood grocery store. My father pulls off the theft while the cashier is busy with another customer. It reminds me of the plot to swipe stilettos from a pawnshop back in Denver. To allay any suspicion my father purchases a pack of Camels and some peanut butter crackers to go with the stolen sardines. Back in our room at the Encino Paradise Motel we dine while watching a detective show featuring MacDonald Carey. I figure the program was probably filmed nearby because a scene involving a car chase occurs on a street that looks identical to the one that stretches past the motel. I suddenly feel like a Hollywood insider.

Bumps and Grinds

THE MANAGER OF THE MOTEL says for me to call him Gary. In my mind he becomes Gary the Gorilla. He chews the end of his cigar as if it were a stick of licorice and repeatedly blinks as though something were poking at his eyes. He and his wife run the place for his brother-in-law, Saul, he says, and they live in an apartment behind the office.

I can help out with the painting, he tells my father, who objects to the idea, observing that I'll get in the way more than help. So Gary says I can hang out by the pool or play miniature golf if I want to. Just as long as I stay out of the way of the paying customers. I'm content to watch television all day long.

The first room my father is to paint is across the courtyard from ours. Gary gives him a pair of paint-spattered overalls that are several sizes too large, and when he emerges from the bathroom with them on, I laugh until I can hardly stand.

"I'm not going to ruin my good clothes," he snaps indignantly, and traipses across the grassy court with the cuffs of the overalls dragging on the ground.

When he's gone I come across some writing paper that has the name of the hotel over a pink flamingo, so I write a letter to my mother for the first time ever to tell her about California. We have a great room with a TV in a fancy motel that has a pool, I tell her, claiming that it is near MacDonald Carey's house.

Later I meet Gary's wife, Doris, in the office when I'm looking for a stamp. When I report that I have written a letter to my mother, she acts as if it is the most wonderful thing she has ever heard and gives me two extra stamps for future letters. Her bluish gray hair is held in place by a scarf whose ends stick up behind her head like Martian antennas. I take her to be pretty old until she starts to dance to a song on the radio, and then she suddenly appears much younger.

"Bet you like rock and roll music, huh? All you kids do. Me too. I was the best boogie-woogier in my high school. Maybe you're a little short on years to appreciate dancing."

She performs several elaborate steps while singing and wagging her finger in time with the music.

"'Get a job. Do da do da do do do do do . . .,' " she squeals off-key.

Gary comes into the office and asks how many cards short of a deck she is today, but she ignores his crack and sings even louder, especially stressing the "do da" parts.

"That's what happens, kid, when your mother drops you on your head when you're a baby," he says, rolling his eyes.

Today he is wearing a shirt that doesn't quite cover his stomach, and the hair in that region is even thicker and longer than on the parts of his body I have seen. It looks as though he has a black wig tucked under his shirt. He retreats to his apartment with his dancing wife in tow, and I go off to locate the mailbox, which Doris has indicated is on the next corner.

On my way I pass a man who I believe is the actor Wendell Corey emerging from a florist shop, but I discount the idea when I see that he is wearing a uniform with a bouquet of flowers embroidered on its breast pocket. Still I reason that maybe he is dressed that way for a role in a movie. After all, he is wearing sunglasses. However, there are no cameras or crew anywhere that I can detect, so I rule out the possibility.

Back at the motel a family comprising three children—a boy and two girls—are loading into a station wagon to begin their day's trip, and the sight of them together and happy arouses envy in me. To have a real family with a father who doesn't drink and works hard to support them and take them on wonderful vacations in a station wagon must be something, I think. No matter, I have a television, I remind myself, and head straight to our room.

During a Tom Terrific cartoon I hear moaning and thumping noises coming from the room next door and feel a vibration as I sit on the bed, whose headboard is flush against the wall. My first thought is that someone is being hurt, maybe a woman, but then I change my mind when I hear giggling. However, when the moaning and thumping intensify, I decide to get my father in case something is actually wrong.

He is in the middle of attempting to move a large bureau when I enter the room he is painting.

"To hell with it!" he exclaims, giving it a kick. "I'll just paint around the goddamn thing. I'm not going to throw my back out for this dump. This is a lousy grind, I can tell you. Not pleasant work with all the paint fumes and this stupid furniture to move."

I report what is happening back at our room and he returns with me. By now the noise is louder and a picture mounted on the wall above my bed looks about to bounce off. I'm especially convinced something strange and terrible is happening when I hear a woman's voice cry, "Oh, God, please! Oh, God!" However, to my surprise, my father has an amused grin on his face.

"Nothing to worry about. Really. Don't pay any attention to it," he says.

When I ask what is going on, he comments that it's just some people exercising. Then he tells me to watch TV and returns to work. The noise abruptly ends in a crescendo of loud sighs, and I have a vague sense that what was going on in the next room is somehow related to what Web did back in Denver and what Joey

Ramone said he saw his brother, Manny, and a girlfriend doing on a couch.

The keyhole in the door that adjoins the two rooms is blocked, so when the racket starts up again a half hour later I do my best to imagine the scene, especially the part when the woman yells out for God.

Another Perfect Family

"WHY THE HELL did you do that?" shouts my father when I mention mailing a letter to my mother. "It'll just get her nuts again," he growls after I ask why he's so upset, but I know he is afraid the cops might catch us.

There are a half-dozen rooms to paint, so we could be at the motel for quite a while and he doesn't need any trouble, he says, adding that maybe he should investigate enrolling me in school. Apparently Gary has asked about my academic situation, and my father has told him that we are waiting for my records to arrive before taking action.

"So just sit tight and don't say anything to anybody, and no more letters. Just watch TV and kind of stay put. People are nosy. We'll get our own place in a while—then you can go to school," he says.

Doris observes that the weather is getting warmer and that it won't be long before things really heat up. It has to do with some kind of a valley or desert wind, she attempts to explain. After she tells me that I look like a younger version of Kookie on 77 *Sunset Strip*, I decide to lie out by the pool and get a tan in case any movie scouts are around. It is there that I meet Bo.

In the middle of a daydream about returning to Albany famous and rich, I hear a voice warning me about getting too much California sun at one time.

"It can fry you real fast. Without knowing it, you're burned to a crisp. Doesn't feel like much until later, but then it hurts like the dickens. Besides, you're starting out a little lighter shade of white than most folks. Hi, I'm Bo. It's short for Bo—ha! You staying here too?" he asks, and extends his hand for me to shake.

He is younger than my father and about the same height but a lot better built. His light brown hair is short and in a cool flattop and his sideburns are neatly trimmed and long. He is what people, especially women, call handsome or cute, and at first I think he may be an aspiring actor like me.

"Yeah, I'm here with my father. He works for the motel. My name's Michael, but most people call me Mike," I answer, and he jokes about what I'm wearing.

"That a dungaree bathing suit? One of them newfangled water fashion jobs?"

I tell him that I'm not going swimming, just sunning, and he says that's a good thing because dungarees absorb so much water that you can hardly move enough to keep from drowning. I tell him that I know that firsthand, since I almost drowned in the Atlantic Ocean last summer, and he continues his discourse on the subject.

"They shrink up too and you know where it really gets you? Right here in the gonads," he says, pointing to his crotch. "Talk about nutcrackers." He laughs. "Now don't tell your dad I said that. He might come looking to give me what for. How old are you?"

"Almost twelve," I tell him, and he says that his stepdaughter, Suzy, is going on nine.

"Maybe I can hook the two of you up. That is, if you like younger women. She's a little cutie. Gonna be a knockout like her mama. Here they come now. We're going sight-seeing," he says as a woman and a little girl approach.

The woman is slightly taller than Bo and has shoulder-length blond hair. She is slender and wears tight pants that run to her calves and a blouse that reveals the smooth skin above her breasts. She's pretty and I think that she and Bo make a perfect Hollywood couple, like Robert Wagner and Natalie Wood, except with lighter hair. The little girl, whose ponytail makes me think of Pamela, stands behind her mother when Bo introduces her.

"This tall beauty is Lucy, and the little beauty is her daughter, Suzy. Ladies, this finely tanned, dungareed young fellow is Michael, but everyone calls him Mike."

"Hiya, Mike," says Lucy, but Suzy remains silent and in her mother's shadow. "Here with your family, hon?"

"Just my father. His name is Curt. Actually, his first name is Fred, or Frederick, but he likes Curt better," I explain, and notice him waving from the doorway of the room he is painting. "That's him over there," I say, pointing in his direction.

Everyone waves back to him, and Bo makes a funny comment about his baggy overalls.

"Say, where are you guys from?" he asks, and I tell him New York State.

He is impressed by this fact and says he's never been right of the Mississippi but plans to get there one of these days.

"Maybe we'll head there next, huh, Lucy? Hey, why don't you and your dad come with us for some Chink food tonight? It's on us. What do you say?" he asks, and Lucy says that would be fun and we could tell them all about New York.

"Hey, Lucy, you like Chinese food?" asks Bo, and she answers that it's one of her favorites. "Well, eat me," he responds, tugging at the corner of his eyes and loudly laughing at his own joke.

"Come with us," says Lucy, giving Bo a hard look. "Suzy would have someone to keep her company for a change besides two old farts."

It sounds great to me, since it beats the scraps we'll have for supper and I've always been curious about Chinese restaurants. I tell them I'll ask my father, and Bo says they'll pick us up around six, after they do some touring and shopping.

My father is not too enthusiastic about the idea but gives in after I work on him for a while.

"Who are these people?" he asks, and I tell him that they're just about the nicest family I have ever met.

Around five-thirty I go looking for my father to remind him about our plans. While he is cleaning the paint from his hands with turpentine, the cigarette in his mouth drops into the can and flames shoot up, catching the bottom of a drape. Before they have a chance to spread, my father manages to stamp them out with his foot. Despite his quick response the drape is slightly damaged.

"Goddamn my rotten luck," he barks, running to the bathroom to empty the flaming can.

When he returns he rearranges a chair and desk so that they cover the evidence of the blaze. As he inspects his handiwork, he lights another cigarette.

"Not bad," he announces, as if he has just created a masterpiece. "Nobody will ever know."

Back in our room my father declares that my hair is hanging over my collar and that I look shabby. It's important to keep up one's appearance, he says. I claim that he is exaggerating how my hair looks, but despite my protests he borrows a pair of scissors from Doris to give me a trim. By the time he has finished, the bathroom floor is covered with dark brown hair.

The result of his labor doesn't look all that good to me when I inspect it in the mirror. After an intense pitch I manage to convince him that his hair is also too long and that it hurts his appearance, and he reluctantly agrees to let me clip some off the back of his neck.

When I accidentally pinch his skin with the scissors as I'm chopping through a thick clump of wavy gray hair, he calls me a damn idiot and yanks them from my hand. There is a trickle of blood where the blades made contact with his flesh, but I don't report this. Besides, the bleeding stops by the time he gets around to putting his shirt back on.

"Forget becoming a barber. Maybe a butcher," he says, slowly overcoming his anger.

When I remind him that I plan to become a radio star or an actor, he says it's too bad I couldn't act like someone with half a brain. Sensing that maybe he has taken his insults too far and is hurting my feelings, he tries his false-teeth joke on me. This time when he tilts his head in the usual silly manner, his plate slips from his mouth onto the bed, and I grab it and run from the room, screaming that I don't want to turn out to be a bum like him and will kill myself if that happens. He is in the doorway yelling at me to come back with his teeth when Bo, Lucy, and Suzy pull into the motel parking lot.

Bo Jester

ON THE RIDE DOWN the boulevard to a place called Lu Chow's, my father hits it off with Bo and Lucy, and by the time we reach our destination they act like long-lost friends. Suzy and I are less chummy, and although she doesn't speak, we do exchange glances. Everything about her reminds me of Pamela, and in a way she is a composite of both my sisters—same nose and mouth, same straight brown hair, same way of staring without really focusing, like she's seeing something that no one else can.

Before we enter the restaurant, Bo stops everybody to show off his new snakeskin boots. I remark that they're beautiful and he says that maybe he'll buy me a pair.

"Makes him taller," says Lucy, and Bo responds that now they can finally see eye to eye.

This sets them both off and we enter Lu Chow's in a gale of laughter.

"Hey, Charlie Chan-san, how about your best table? You sell burgers and pizza here?" he teases the Chinese host.

"No plizza. No hambligga," responds the old man without a trace of humor.

The way he speaks delights Bo, who mimics his pronunciations several times as we're escorted to our table. This amuses everyone, but not half as much as it does Bo himself.

"How about some firewater, Curt? You like that wine made of

that Minute rice stuff? They heat it up and it goes down like liquid fire. It can take the fuzz off your testes. Let's get this party rolling," he says, and I throw my father a warning look.

"Not me," he says, and Bo asks if he's on the wagon.

Before my father comes up with an answer, Bo says that he's been on the wagon before too, but only until it reached the bar.

I have never seen such huge menus and haven't the slightest idea of what to order or how much, and I can tell from my father's face that he doesn't either. This isn't a problem for long because Bo orders for all of us. When he tells the waitress what we want, I think he is making another joke, but when she gives him a matter-of-fact nod and repeats, "Poop-poop platter for six," my concern shifts to what this distasteful-sounding dish consists of.

"Suzy loves to eat poop-poop, right honey?" says Bo, laughing, and she gives him a polite smile. "Of course, it makes her poop all night," he continues, trying unsuccessfully to get a rise out of her, and I wonder why she is so unresponsive.

Lucy fishes through her pocketbook for her cigarettes and when she can't locate them my father offers her one of his. As she is about to accept, Bo takes a pack of Salems from his shirt pocket and hands it to her.

"What you doing with my cigarettes, sugar? Am I driving you to smoke?" she asks. "No, only to drink," says Bo. He flips the lid of his Zippo with one hand and lights her cigarette.

"Why, thank you, kind sir," she says, taking an extravagantly deep drag.

I notice my father looking at her with a peculiar glint in his eyes and wonder what is on his mind. Does she remind him of his platinum blond stepmother? I wonder. My curiosity increases when I see her returning the same look to him. This union goes on for about ten seconds until there is a loud pop and a puff of smoke in front of her face. Bo laughs hysterically.

"Loaded your butt, honey," he says, about to fall off his seat.

Lucy appears somewhat dazed and mortified as the paper from

the detonated cigarette sticks to her blackened mouth like a daisy in full bloom. The absurd sight makes everyone but Suzy laugh, including the Chinese busboy, who is chuckling so hard he spills the water intended for our glasses onto the tablecloth.

"You could have hurt me. I think my eyebrows are singed," she complains, inspecting herself in the mirror of her compact.

This comment makes us laugh even harder.

"Maybe I'll stick some of those caps up your butt," she remarks to Bo, and this actually causes him to fall off his chair.

By the time the food arrives, the laughter has died down to only an occasional eruption when Bo makes a popping sound with his tongue and impersonates Lucy's startled expression. Meanwhile she has cleaned her face and added fresh makeup to her lips and cheeks, but there are still telltale signs of the explosion. This prank has cooled her mood, although later in the meal she becomes more like her former self.

My father has managed to resist Bo's urgings that he join him in drinking the Asian alcohol he has ordered, and I have succeeded in devouring as many spareribs and chicken wings as my bound intestines will tolerate. When we are given fortune cookies, Bo immediately opens his and reads it aloud.

"You will have happy long life with beautiful blond," he recites, and Lucy rubs his hand affectionately. "After you dump current blond," he adds, and Lucy pulls at the hairs on his arm.

"Who else wants their fortunes read?" he asks while opening another cookie. "This one's yours, Curt. Wise man say he who paint only what eye can see is hiding much."

This gets my father's attention, but before he can respond, Bo reveals that they are in one of his recently painted rooms and that when he moved a dresser to retrieve something that fell behind it, he discovered the unpainted section.

"A little earth tremor, and your gig is up," he says with a smirk.

When my father refers to the problem with his bad back, Bo says he shouldn't worry about it because he's saving the motel owner money on paint.

"Anyway, I bet you ain't getting overpaid. Those kikes are all the same. Tight as a virgin when it comes to a buck, or is that a fuck," remarks Bo, and Lucy tells him to watch his mouth around the kids.

"Didn't say *fuck*. I said *buck*, or was it *suck?*" he whispers loud enough for everyone to hear, and Lucy pinches him.

"You're like an overgrown kid sometimes," she says, half laughing.

The check arrives and Bo removes his wallet. My father makes a gesture to reach for his, but much to his relief Bo waves him off.

"This is our treat, remember?" he says, allowing the plastic holder in his wallet to flop open. "We got lots of credit cards and a whole pile of checks to buy all the rice in China. Don't we, baby?" he says to Lucy, grabbing her by the waist. "So what say we break in a new one? What d'you think, Curt?"

My father is impressed but there is a trace of skepticism in his eyes.

"Car-tee Blan-chee is a good one," he says, playfully pronouncing the exotic words on the small plastic card. "What all the big shots have. Except maybe one." He winks complicitly at Lucy. "You can just about buy a yacht with this one, and maybe that's just what we'll do tomorrow. Want to take a cruise with us, you guys?" he asks, and we say sure.

"I got a better idea," he continues. "How about tomorrow we buy Mike here an honest-to-God bathing suit and maybe some new kicks. Looks like the ones you're wearing have run out of gas. What about you, Curt? Bet you could use something. How about a pair of overalls that fit? Just kidding, buddy. Our treat, right, Lucy?"

She thinks it's a great idea and after some hesitation my father agrees to the shopping spree.

"Charge!" shouts Bo, and we leave Lu Chow's.

Jail Bait

BO AND LUCY are not early risers, but Suzy is. As I monitor the door to their room from ours, I see her emerge with roller skates attached to her feet. She is unsteady and clutches at the wall as she moves down the cement walkway. She has left the door to the room ajar and the wind opens it further. Inside the dark interior I discern Bo standing on top of a bed in his undershorts. He is doing what looks like some kind of exotic dance when Lucy appears from the room's inner recesses. She is topless and has on skimpy black panties. As Bo gyrates she tugs at his shorts and he topples on top of her, pushing both of them out of sight except for their intertwined legs, which flail about.

Suzy skates up to the door, looks inside, and moves on as if she has seen nothing out of the ordinary. My father is working in a unit two doors down from theirs and when she passes he waves, but she does not return his greeting.

From our window I also have a view of the empty motel office and part of the pool area. Gary is skimming the water's surface with a long pole, an indication that he expects a busy day.

"When the hot winds start blowing, people sometimes check in just to use the pool and cool off. That happened a lot last summer because it was sizzling. All they used the rooms for was to change into their swimsuits and maybe do a little clutching afterward. Half the time we didn't even have to change the beds," observed Gary to my father when we were standing by the pool a half hour earlier.

It is approaching noon by the time Bo and Lucy are ready to go shopping. My father tells Gary he is taking off a few hours to check out the local schools for me, and we're on our way. Lucy says my father is good-looking for a man over fifty, and Bo tells him to watch out for her because she is what he calls a nympho.

"Can't get enough of it," he says, and she responds that he must be talking about himself.

Our first stop is a department store in downtown Encino. Lucy writes a check for a leather purse and several pairs of nylons, and Bo tries on a plaid sport coat but decides that it is not jazzy enough for him.

"How about we go down to Hollywood? They've got tons of stores," suggests Lucy, and this is fine with everyone, particularly me.

During the next couple of hours we each end up with a parcel as we scour the shops along the famous city's main thoroughfare. Bo has written a check for a fancy western shirt with buttons that look like pearls and he says tonight we all should go high-stepping the way they do back in Odessa, Texas, his hometown.

"My daddy used to call the steps at barn dances. I went with him when I was visiting from my mom's place in Little Rock. I remember once he got sloshed as an Injun and started messing up and giving the wrong calls. You never saw so much confusion in your life. Folks on the dance floor looked like compasses in a magnet factory. They were ziggin' and zaggin' every which way. Couple whacked heads and were out cold for twenty minutes, and I ain't making that up neither."

Suzy has a new doll and dress and I have a pair of blue Keds and swim trunks. My father has steadfastly refused to let anything be bought for him other than a carton of Camels and a handkerchief set. The latter has been purchased for him by Bo, who calls the gift a humane act, given the way my father attacks his nose with his deformed finger.

"Prying at the ole schnoz with your stub like that spreads it out so you end up looking like one of them duck-billed platter-pussies," he explains as my father listens stoically. "When you blow it instead of picking it, you end up squeezing all the snots out. That keeps it from getting humongous, although in your case, Curt, it may be a little too late. By the look of that nose of yours it ain't been touched by anything but your finger since your mama washed your face when you was in short pants."

Everyone laughs, including my father, who tries to take Bo's ribbing in stride. One part of me finds his comments funny, but another part of me wants to tell him to shut up and leave my father alone because I know his feelings are hurt and I feel sorry for him.

On our way back to the car we see a small crowd gathered in front of a jewelry store and we check it out. The attraction turns out to be Dean Jagger, and Lucy gets an autograph and flirts with the actor while Bo tells him that he sure did a good job in some movie Bo saw. He can't remember its title, so the actor mentions a few, but none sounds familiar. Although I can't recall seeing him in anything, I'm excited to be standing so close to someone everyone else seems to recognize.

My father asks him if he knew his uncle and namesake, Frederick Curtis, who supposedly was a hotshot booking agent in New York in the 1930s. Mr. Jagger says the name sounds familiar and this pleases my father, who then claims that Jack Dempsey was a client of his uncle's.

"Didn't he set up shop out here for a while?" asks the actor, and my father says that indeed he did work out here until his accident.

"That's right—he died in a freak accident, as I recall. I think I remember reading about it in *Variety*. A bottle or jar fell on him in a grocery market, right?"

My father tells him that it was actually an entire display of stewed tomatoes that came crashing down on him when he was stooped over, and Bo adds that the old guy should have known better than to take something from the bottom of the stack.

We bid Mr. Jagger farewell and on our way to the car Lucy claims the actor had the hots for her, adding that the bigger they are the nicer they are. On the drive back to the motel I savor the view of the famous hillside letters that denote this celebrated town and am filled with the hope of someday being asked for my own autograph.

When I announce to the carload that I'm going to be a movie star when I grow up, my father remarks that I better get into something more practical, like sales. Bo suggests that I look into something he has heard about called computers, which are machines that do the work for people, he claims.

"Pretty soon robots are going to be doing everything, so it's a smart idea to learn how they work because it's for certain that they'll need humans to repair them."

"Well, if they're so great, why can't they fix themselves?" remarks Lucy, who says that she thinks I'd make a great actor and that I should do what I want to do in life and not listen to a couple of know-it-alls.

After my father goes back to work I put on my new swim trunks and go to join Bo, Lucy, and Suzy by the pool. On my way Gary stops me and tells me that there are guests there, so I shouldn't use it. He reminds me what he said about staying out of the way of the paying customers. My heart sinks and I suddenly feel like a nobody. When I tell him that they invited me to take a swim with them, he says it would be better if I just let them enjoy the pool alone. With these words I turn to go back to my room, but Bo shouts for me, and Gary reluctantly nods for me to go ahead. Still my mood has been shot full of holes and I feel like I don't belong at the Encino Paradise Motel, where guests have privileges that kids of lowly room painters are not entitled to.

Bo is teaching Suzy how to swim by holding her above the water as she flaps her arms and legs. One of his hands is under her legs and the other is under her chest. There is a look of mild discomfort on her face and after a couple of minutes she tells him that she doesn't want to learn how to swim today.

Lucy is sunbathing in a lounge chair, and from where I stand in the shallow end of the pool I can see tiny brown hairs sticking out of the bottom of her bathing suit. Bo catches me looking and jokes that Lucy's a little too mature for me to handle but that little Suzy might be just about right. With that comment he hoists her above the water and slides his hand between her legs.

"Nice little box," he whispers in my direction, and Suzy squirms to break his hold.

When he slips his fingers inside her swimsuit she calls for her mother, who says for everyone to pipe down because she is trying to get her beauty rest. Then she yells at Bo to stop teasing Suzy and to act his age. He reluctantly releases the girl, commenting that maybe I should teach her how to swim, but I admit that I don't know how myself.

A little while later we're forced to leave the pool area because of an approaching thunderstorm, and I accompany the group back to their room. Once there, Bo makes the comment to Lucy that I have an eye for her, and she says that while I may be a little on the young side, I'm sure cuter than most of the guys she's gone out with, Bo included.

She plops down on the bed in her bathing suit and grabs my arm, telling me to sit on her lap. I hesitate, but she pulls me onto her.

"Hey there, big fella," she says flirtatiously. "You got something you want to show me?" And with that she touches my crotch.

"Lucy, honey, I think you're making him blush. His face is red as a beet," says Bo with a wide, toothy smile.

"You embarrassed?" asks Lucy, maintaining her hand on my lap. "I'm not gonna eat you up, sweetie, or maybe I will."

"Hey, Mike, ever get a hard-on?" asks Bo, and Lucy says for him to shut up because he's scaring me, and with that she removes her hand from me.

"Poor thing's trembling. Don't mind him, baby. He's just a little crazy at times."

"Pussy-crazy," he responds, and I attempt to slip from Lucy's embrace, saying that I'm going to my room to watch the *Mickey Mouse Club,* but she draws me closer to her so that my head is against her breasts.

"Now, Mike, you're getting what other guys have to pay for, so enjoy it," remarks Bo, and Lucy tells him to shut up.

"Maybe he is a tad on the young side," says Lucy, releasing me.

"Well, I'm not, sweetcakes," says Bo, removing the wet towel from around his waist and revealing what he calls his hot rod. "So why don't you come scrub my bumper while I take a shower? Then you can scrub my hood ornament too."

I say good-bye on my way to the door and Lucy asks if it's okay if Suzy comes with me. Bo arches his eyebrow, shoots me a mischievous smile, and moves his finger back and forth in his cupped hand. It is a gesture I have seen others use, mostly older kids, and I don't have any doubt as to its meaning.

"You be careful what you do with that little girl. She's jailbait. Course I suppose you are too," says Bo as he dashes naked to the bathroom.

While we watch TV, Suzy sits huddled on the corner of my father's bed and only removes the thumb from her mouth long enough to report that Karen is her favorite Mouseketeer.

Retribution

A FEW DAYS pass without our seeing much of Bo and Lucy, whom my father has nicknamed the Check-and-Charge-Its. They are still registered at the motel, says Doris, adding that they said something about going down to Tijuana but should be back anytime. When they do return they are in a hurry to check out and within minutes have packed their things into their car and are gone without saying good-bye.

There must be something wrong, I tell my father as we watch their car pull out of the parking lot, and he says that they are probably on the run from the cops.

"Phony checks and credit cards, I bet," he comments, slightly slurring his words.

A closer inspection of his eyes and a deep whiff of his breath confirms my suspicion.

"You've been drinking," I say, and he shakes his head as if to say I am hallucinating. "I hate you and I hate California too. This place isn't so great. Nothing ever turns out good with you," I add vengefully, shooting him my most ferocious look.

"What are you yapping about now? You're the one who couldn't wait to get here. California this, California that . . . Jesus! Now it's not so hot, huh? I just gargled with some Listerine. That's what you smell. Not booze. A lot you know, mister."

"You liar!" I shout, and when he turns and starts to walk away I lunge at him and strike his shoulder blade with my fist.

The moment I do this my desire to decimate him is gone and replaced by remorse and concern that I may have hurt him. He is rocked by my surprise attack and I sense he is about to retaliate. I run to our room, hoping to reach it and lock him out, but before I get to the door he grabs me by the collar and slaps my head, causing my ear to burn and ring. His mouth is twisted in anger and the veins in his forehead are visible. Fear mixed with regret reduces me to tears and I throw my arms around him and apologize.

"Are you okay, Dad?" I ask between sobs, and he says never to hit him again.

"It's a hell of a thing to punch your own father like that. You know what my old man would have done? He would have belted me for a lot less than what you did, I can tell you. You just don't do that sort of thing. It's not right. You know my back is bad too," he says, and I feel even worse.

We continue to embrace for a moment inside the doorway of our room. This level of affection is unfamiliar to us and there is an awkwardness as we move to our respective parts of the room.

"Don't worry—I'm not going to start drinking, Butch. I just took a little nip for medicinal purposes because my back's been kind of sore from all the damn painting," he says, rubbing his shoulder blade where my fist landed. "The ceilings are a killer. That's what I've been doing the last couple of days. Makes my back real jumpy. It's a hard job, you know. Knocks you out, and I'm not exactly a kid. You just watch TV and sit by the pool all day long while I'm working my ass off," he says, fishing for more sympathy.

When he returns to work I search the room for any liquor that he may have hidden. In the corner of the closet I find an empty Thunderbird wine bottle, which he later claims he has never seen.

"Probably left there by someone before we got the room. Maybe Frank Belrose. I need some rest, so stop the damn nagging," he says, and his speech and manner have a fuzziness that comes from something other than fatigue.

"Yeah, the tooth fairy left it," I reply, and he snickers.

"You're something. Never know when to shut up. Besides, if I want a drink it's none of your business. You're just a kid, not a grown-up. Start acting your age," he says, lying back on his bed.

"You don't even *know* my age," I snap back, and he waves me off as he turns over and pulls the covers over his head.

"You think I don't know that it's your birthday?" he says smugly. This is the first time he has acknowledged the fact.

"Happy birthday, Butch. We'll get you something later," he mumbles into his pillow before falling into an inebriated slumber.

The Cover-Up

"CURT, YOU son of a bitch! . . . Curt!"

Gary's shouting and pounding at our door wake us with a start. My father pulls on his pants and opens the door the length of its chain lock. Before he has a chance to utter a word, Gary pushes his shoulder against the door and the lock snaps apart. He is in the room instantly and waving his fist at my father and accusing him of being a crook.

"You think I'm some kind of dumb schmuck or something? What kind of shit are you trying to pull? You better be out of here in twenty minutes or I'll call the cops on you."

My father tells Gary that he's upset over nothing and that he planned to paint all the spaces behind the furniture.

"I was going to go back and finish when I got done with the ceilings. My back was bothering me, so I figured I'd do it later. Now I'm okay and I can move furniture. Only take a couple of days," he says, trying to bring Gary's temperature down a notch, but Gary is steaming mad and not buying any of it.

"Bullshit! Just get your asses out of here before I come back. You hear me?" he says, his furry arm inches from my father's face.

Try as he may, my father is unable to defuse Gary's wrath and when he senses that he is getting nowhere he becomes indignant and hostile.

"Hey, I been working my ass off for you. You can't just bounce me and the kid out on the street. It's Sunday, for Christ's sake. Where the hell will we go? You owe me money."

Gary says my father can go piss up a rope as far as he is concerned and that if anything he is the one owed money. My father curses him, and this further incites Gary, who invites my father to step outside to settle the score. He moves from the doorway to the grass across the walkway and beckons my father, who stands his ground inside the room.

"Come on—let's see who's the cocksucker," shouts Gary, who in his current rage resembles a human-size version of King Kong to me. He'd gladly join him, says my father, but he's not about to re-injure his back over such stupid shit as this.

"You get out of here or I'll kick your goy ass and then call the police. They'd probably be interested in the situation with the kid, you friggin' boozer," yells Gary, and my father flips him the finger and slams the door shut, putting the back of a chair under the knob in case Gary should come storming in after him.

"Ten minutes!" screams Gary, and as he stomps away several guests of the motel peek out of their room windows.

"Jew bastard! They're all alike," spits my father, and we gather our few possessions.

I feel profound regret at having to leave such posh accommodations and wonder if we'll ever have a room with a television again.

"You shouldn't have painted around the furniture," I say as we slip around the corner of the motel to avoid another encounter with Gary the Gorilla.

"Now don't tell me what I should have done. What I should have done was leave you with your friggin' old lady," he replies, and I tell him he's right and that I'd be better off with her and that California stinks anyway as we move down the quiet boulevard.

"She's better than you," I yell back at him, reminding him again that I thought the Golden State was going to be better than it has turned out and that there are probably a lot of better places to be and that I intend to go and find them.

"Well, your old lady's no bargain either, kiddo. Did she write you a letter back? No! You should have heard from her by now," he says, and noticing the hurt on my face, he tries to mitigate the bite of his comment.

"You probably got the address wrong, Butch. Did you put a return address on the envelope?"

No, I say, adding that she would never forget to answer my letter because she's not like him. This renews his irritation.

"Well, go back with her. I don't need you. You're just a pain in the ass like she is, like all women are. Nothing but trouble my whole lousy life. We might as well get a ride back east. You can go live with your mother and sisters. Maybe you'll be happier there. Things just haven't worked out."

The idea doesn't sound all that bad to me. California truly has lost much of its appeal. It is not the place I imagined it to be. It's kind of a disappointment. If there are movie stars here, they stay hidden, except for Dean Jagger, who really isn't that big of a star anyway. Suddenly I feel a torrent of emotion. "I thought it would be better here in California, but it's not," I say, gulping for air between heavy sobs. "I want to leave. I just want to go." For the rest of my childhood on the road with my father I would realize that our destinations were never as thrilling as the travels to them.

By late morning we're on Route 66 and my mood has improved. It feels good to be back out on the highway and moving on to somewhere else. We have charted our return trip on our shaggy road map, whose northwestern panel has fallen off and is missing.

"Good thing we're not bumming a ride to Oregon," jokes my father, lighting a cigarette and peering tentatively in the direction of an oncoming car.

Our next stop is to be Las Vegas and for me that magic-sounding place takes some of the sting out of traveling in an easterly direction. My father figures he can probably get some quick work there with all the hotels.

"We'll find a place to lay our heads for a couple of weeks till I make some cash," he says. "Then maybe I'll just put you on the bus for Albany."

But already I'm thinking about a detour to Florida, the Sunshine State, the land his father helped develop. He says the season is over down there, so we might as well just head east for the time being. We still have plenty of West to go through, so I'm in no hurry. It would be great to see Texas, I say, and my father remarks that it may be the biggest state but that there's really nothing there.

"Plenty of wide-open spaces," I offer, as if that will entice him, and he remarks that you can't eat open spaces.

At the moment I would like something to fill the wide-open space in my stomach, which feels like it is pushing in on itself.

PART V
LOS ANGELES TO LAS VEGAS
(275 Miles)

Mojave-Bound

THE JOY OF MOTION has revived me and it helps mitigate my discomforting hunger and intestinal roadblock. Two rides take us as far as Barstow, a town just to the south of Death Valley. Las Vegas is still another 150 miles away and it is getting late in the day. As usual my father is unnerved by the prospect of nightfall in a desolate location. I tell him we can make it as far as the next town, Baker, which is another 50 miles closer to our destination, but he wants to pull in for the night. It's too risky, he says, with a look that would give anyone the impression that he has just discounted the idea of going over Niagara Falls in a barrel.

He has nine dollars and some change and we take a room in a small, dilapidated hotel that requires most of it. "They got you where they want you in this cow town," complains my father, upset with what he feels is an exorbitant price for such dingy accommodations in a one-horse burg. By the time we consume the morsels of what constitutes our supper we're down to a little more than a buck, and my father wants to scout out a Catholic church just in case.

The radiator in our room clanks and hisses most of the night, contributing to my father's insomnia, he contends. At one point even I'm awakened by the racket and I see him sitting in the window shooting the beam of his flashlight into the darkness. When he senses that I'm watching him he reports that it is colder than an Eskimo's fanny outside and says for me to go back to sleep.

"The desert can be an oven during the day and a Deepfreeze at night," he says, pressing his open palm against the glass.

When I wake up in the morning, he is still seated at the window. The bright sun makes it look warmer but when my bare feet touch the floor it feels like ice. The accumulated dirt and sweat in my tattered socks has formed them into a crusty shell, and I have to rub and smack them against the metal leg of the bed to soften them. Despite everything I do, it is still like walking barefoot on stale crusts of bread. Meanwhile I notice that the dirt on the nubs of my anklebones has hardened to the point that digging at them with my fingernails has little effect. These souvenirs of privation I will wear into early adulthood.

My father has coffee and I have a powdered doughnut and a glass of water before we walk to the edge of town to begin our day of thumbing. The wind bulldozes us as we move up Route 66, and as usual my father has a few choice words to say about that. A half mile or so out of the town center we start hitching. The location we have chosen is perfect because it gives would-be rides an opportunity to slow down and pull off onto a wide shoulder. Since we're outside Barstow and beyond the reach of its modest suburbs, any ride we catch is likely to be going at least as far as the next populated area, dozens of miles away.

The desert stretches to the horizon in all directions, and my father calls the place the end of the earth as he nervously jingles the pennies in his pocket. When a particularly strong blast of arid wind stirs the dust and sand around us, he becomes highly agitated and says as far as he's concerned the Indians can have the stinking place. What Indians? I ask, and he says whatever friggin' Indians are dumb enough to live out here.

Only occasionally does a car pass, and then more often than not it is a military vehicle.

"This is just great," laments my father, his frustration mounting. "It's against the rules for these guys to pick up civilians, so we're never going to get a ride."

The longer we stand on the lonely stretch of highway, the warmer the sun gets, and by late morning we have shed our Denver thrift shop coats. The gusts are less frequent but when they occur it is with extraordinary force, and each time this happens my father becomes unglued and threatens to quit for the day. I suggest we pretend to be in a movie about two guys stranded on the desert and he looks at me in utter disgust.

To needle him as much as to embellish my scenario, I make the sound of howling wind, and when we're nearly blown off our feet by a sudden explosion of air, he yells at me to stop as if I am its cause.

Around noon we head back into town to get something to drink and some peanut butter or cheese crackers for lunch. Just as we're about to abandon our spot, a car pulls over. We are delighted, but when we begin to run in its direction it peels away, pelting us with stones and gravel from its spinning tires. This angers me more than it does my father and when I shout an expletive at the fading vehicle my father makes the sound of howling wind as if to even the score with me.

Moon and the Misbegotten

WE RETURN TO THE highway and stand there for hours. Our faces are coated with blown sand, and my father complains of having half of the damn desert in his eyes.

"At this rate I'll be blind by the time we get out of this shit hole," he gripes, digging at his bloodshot eyes.

When I drag my fingernail across my cheek I leave a groove that I'm sure resembles a gruesome scar. My father tells me to leave my face alone because if we look any worse than we do already, we'll never get a ride. Not that we're ever going to get one anyway, he adds, flicking what he has dug from his eye at the road.

Without having had so much as a hint of someone stopping for us, we finally throw in the towel and head back into Barstow. Just a couple of blocks from the center of town we locate a Catholic church and rectory and tap on its door. A short, round figure in a crisp white T-shirt and black pants asks us in. He is the rector, he explains, and doesn't look any too happy about that fact. I wonder if he hates being out in the middle of nowhere as much as my father does or is just tired of seeing bums like us.

My father tells the priest that we are awaiting a letter with money in it from my mother, which should reach us by general delivery at the local post office in a day or two, and are stranded until then. This gets us a furnished, two-room apartment owned by a parishioner, and a charge account at a nearby grocery store run by another.

The little apartment is cozy and clean and overlooks the highway we have come to know all too well. We shop for food and much to his chagrin my father is told that he can't charge cigarettes. Outside the store he calls this a stupid rule, reasoning that he eats less because he smokes, so this more than balances things out.

That night we pass the time watching the sparse traffic as it moves down the moonlit road toward places we would much rather be. My suggestion that we stand in front of the house and try our luck at getting a ride, since we have nothing better to do, is soundly rejected.

"Yeah, and get dropped off in the middle of nowhere? Why do you think they call it Death Valley? No, thanks," says my father, shaking his head and pursing his chapped lips as though he has just sucked on a lemon.

"The moon is so bright it looks like day outside," I counter, but he says if people won't pick us up in the daylight they sure as hell aren't going to stop for us in the moonlight.

"Besides," he says, "it's a full moon and that makes people kind of nutty. All we need to do is get a ride from some wacko out there in the middle of the desert. God knows what would happen."

When I concentrate my gaze at the man in the moon, he seems to be grinning at every word that comes from my father's mouth.

"You're just afraid of werewolves," I say, and he replies that my comment is ridiculous, then proceeds to remove his flashlight from our bag.

"You can't kill them with that," I respond, goading him.

"No, but you can blind them long enough to get away," he says, flashing the beam of light in my face and cackling like a dope.

Each time a car passes, the glow from its headlights dances across the room and I follow the path of this ceiling traffic until it leads me to sleep. In the morning my father determines that we need to scrape the desert off our bodies because if we look any worse we will never get picked up. Checking my image in the mirror, I conclude that we almost look like colored people.

"And you think anybody out there is going to give a ride to a couple of coons?" he snaps.

"They might think we're Amos 'n' Andy," I say, and he tells me to clamp it and remove the grime on me.

My father doesn't like actual baths and I've never know him to take one, but he does give himself plenty of what he calls sponge baths. This involves stripping down to his T-shirt and scrubbing his face, neck, and arms with a washrag. Soap is optional as long as the cloth is nice and wet. He usually concludes his cleansing ritual by dousing his head with the mucky remains in the sink. His hair dripping, he swiftly combs it back in place and pats dry the accumulated moisture from the back of his head and neck. If he has any Old Spice or Mennen aftershave lotion, he splashes handfuls under his armpits and occasionally in the crotch of his pants or undershorts.

"It's important to keep clean," he proclaims after his watery ablutions. "You get nowhere in this world if you look or smell cruddy. Now sponge off like I did."

"Maybe I'll take a real bath," I say, and he tells me not to be stupid, adding that we don't have any towels, only the worn-out washrag he has just used, and besides, we have to get going.

While I engage in my own sponge bath I spy him secretly applying his Maybelline stick to his eyebrows—the finishing touch in his quest to restore his youth and reverse the decay of his appearance.

Severed Butts

WE ARE SOON at our designated launching site, following a repast of undercooked boiled eggs and instant coffee that my father doles out sparingly because he claims that caffeine is not good for kids. We retain the keys to the apartment in the event that we have to return, a possibility I block from my thoughts.

"If we get a ride, we'll mail the keys back to the priest," says my father, but I know that is unlikely.

It is another brilliantly clear day and not as cold as yesterday morning, although the air has a frosty edge to it. Approximately fifty yards from the opposite side of the highway are railroad tracks, and a couple of times a day a long freight train passes us heading east. It moves so slowly that I calculate it would be easy to hop, and there are many cars with open doors. My father enumerates the dangers of doing this. We could fall under the wheels, get locked inside a refrigerated car, be arrested by railroad dicks, run into hostile hoboes, and so forth, he says, so he doesn't want any part of my scheme.

Later in the morning a train rolls by and I make a pitch for jumping on board. "We can do it easy. Maybe it's going all the way to New York. We could be stuck here forever," I say, but my father is adamant, saying there is no way he's going to lose his legs or life to get a few lousy miles. Then he tells me about an old photograph in a *National Geographic* he once saw of a Sioux Indian whose severed body lay across a track after he'd tried to jump onto a passing train.

"His eyes were still open and they looked like they were staring back at his cutoff ass and legs," he says, pausing for added emphasis. "Besides, that damn freight train is probably only going as far as the next hick town," he continues, and I point out that several of its cars are marked CHESAPEAKE LINE, which I know is the name of a place back east.

When the train has meandered beyond the point of capture, I invoke my howling-wind sound effect, but the air is calm, so it doesn't have quite the impact it did the day before.

Around noon we go back to the apartment for a drink and something to eat. Back at our spot on the road my father hints at quitting for the day.

"We're getting too much sun and that's probably not good. Besides, someone might see us who knows the priest or landlady, and that would cause trouble," he says.

I think he has a point about the sun's being dangerous. My forehead and nose are burning and sore to the touch. This will turn out to be one of my father's few prescient moments, because when I am an adult my overexposure to the sun will result in several basal cell skin cancers, which will have to be excavated from my damaged flesh.

Beyond the railroad tracks a convincing mirage transforms the desert into a great, inviting lake. In the middle of the undulating illusion I discern a busy city street filled with people and traffic.

My father says that he read somewhere that mirages are really reflections of other places far away created by gases in the atmosphere, and then he lets out a resounding fart and tells me I should now be able to see a few more streets.

We stay put for a couple more hours, but not long after he has smoked his last cigarette my father insists we go back into town. Back at our lodgings, after counting his change my father despairs over being a few pennies shy of a pack of cigarettes. By now he is having withdrawal symptoms and wondering how he might persuade the grocery store to bend its silly rules on this one occasion.

He tries to bargain with the store manager, telling him that as soon as the money arrives in the mail he will reimburse him, but nothing convinces the man to modify his position.

"Sorry, but cigarettes are classified as a luxury item, like nylons or cosmetics, and we just don't allow people on church accounts to charge such goods," says the aproned grocer, whose very shoulder is inches from the cigarette display case mounted above the cash register.

"The bastard! You'd think I was asking for caviar," my father complains bitterly when we're outside.

On Barstow's main street he scans the sidewalks for partially smoked cigarettes and pretends to be tying his shoelace when bending to scoop them up. I do likewise and listen to him as he condemns people who smoke filter-tipped cigarettes.

"Jerks smoke them right down to the filters so there's nothing left. How can that be better for you? You're actually smoking more than with regular cigarettes."

We continue to troll the pavement until our pockets are filled with used butts. Just as he is about to light the longest of the bunch, he notices lipstick on it, so he puts the burned end between his lips for sanitary purposes, I assume.

As usual the first drag raises his spirits and he suggests we check to see if there's an AA in town. It turns out there is a listing in the phone book, so my father dials the number and arranges for someone to take us to a meeting held that night at an air force base outside Barstow.

"Kill some time anyway, Butch. Better than staring out the stupid window at idiots who wouldn't give God himself a ride."

For our evening meal we have a concoction consisting of badly scrambled eggs and sardines in mustard sauce that my father refers to as a seafood omelette, and at about six o'clock the ride to our evening's entertainment arrives.

When my father peeks out the window in response to the honking of a horn, he lets out a loud groan. Parked in front is a pickup truck that looks as if it has been unearthed by a team of archaeologists.

Seeing the Light

WE HEAD SOUTH across the desert with a guy named Gunther Purdue to the AA meeting held at a remote military base.

"Call me Gun. Not as hoity-toity as Gunther. My mom named me after some duke or lord she read about in a dime novel. Never fancied it much, but Gun I can live with," he says, and then proceeds to tell us his life story as we bounce along an occasionally paved but mostly gravel road.

He has been sober for more than a year, he reports, adjusting his cap so that its frayed and discolored visor nearly touches his nose, forcing him to tip his head back to see the road. "The longest I been dry since I was sixteen, and I'm twenty-nine now," he tells us.

It is about thirty miles down the patchy road to the base, which rises from the empty horizon like a small city on the moon. Gunther tells us that there are mostly civilians at these meetings. "Folks as far away as Amboy and Kelso come over. Mostly ranchers. Think all this desert out here gives a person a mighty thirst. Can't help wanting something to drink all the time. Some of these fellas live where there's not another soul within fifty miles, so the bottle becomes their best friend."

Before the meeting gets under way the person running it, a senior airman, E-4, Gun tells us, gets the idea that it would be amusing if I got up in front of the group and told about my addiction to soda pop. I agree to go along with the joke, and when he introduces me I ad-lib a story about being hooked on root beer and how it made me lose all my toys and flunk math. The crowd is entertained by my performance, and my father has a smug look on his face. I get the biggest applause of the night and he tells me not to let it go to my head.

"A real little ham," he tells Gun, who shakes my hand enthusiastically when I return to my seat.

A woman about my mother's age and build is introduced next and moves to the front of the room. She is clearly quite apprehensive and uncomfortable being in the spotlight and when she takes a sip of water from a glass on the podium, it goes down the wrong way, causing her to choke. When she regains her composure she begins her sad tale.

"Well, my name is Gloria and I'm an alcoholic," she says, adding that she has been sober for one year, four months, and eleven days.

Her drinking, she says, caused her to lose her family and do things that no self-respecting woman would ever do.

Two more AA members tell equally compelling stories about their lives under the destructive influence of alcohol, but my father appears preoccupied and bored. Later, as usual, he distances himself from the people at the meeting as if their drinking problems have nothing to do with his life. In fact he heartily denies having a drinking problem, let alone being an alcoholic.

When the subject comes up back in the apartment, he repeats his claim that he is a social drinker, admitting that he may overdo it at times.

"I can stop whenever I want, though, and I always have," he boasts, and I am frustrated by this absolutely absurd statement.

Following the meeting there is coffee and doughnuts—one of our reasons for coming. The cigarettes my father has managed to bum from several people are the other. In record time I gulp down two cream-filled doughnuts and one covered with a bright orange glaze. By the time we leave, my stomach feels like a cement block.

We make the trip back to Barstow in total darkness, and when I remark about this, Gun turns off the headlights to demonstrate just how dark it really is. Before he puts them back on there is a series of thumping and crunching sounds from under the truck.

"Jackalopes," says Gun, and when he restores the headlights the road before us is covered with large rabbits, which appear frozen in their tracks by the two bright shafts of light coming from the truck.

"Hypnotizes 'em," he explains, and I'm astonished and horrified that he doesn't stop or even slow down. "Nothin' you can do but run 'em over. So darn many of 'em and stubborn as all get-out. Won't get out of the way if you do stop. Unless you want to be stuck out here till sunrise, you just gotta flatten the poor critters."

The noise of the rabbits being crushed by the truck's tires makes my guts churn and I feel like heaving up. My father's demeanor reveals that he is not enjoying the massacre either.

When I announce that I'm on the verge of puking, Gun suggests that I ride in back of the pickup, where I can hang off and throw up as much as I want. When he stops the truck and I climb out to make the switch, my feet touch the carcass of a freshly mangled rabbit and all the doughnuts in my stomach fly past my lips. Unfortunately most of what gushes from me lands on the door of the truck. This doesn't faze Gun, who says that it will blow off on the way back to town.

For the balance of the ride I huddle in the open bed of the pickup with my hands pressed hard against my ears to keep from hearing the slaughter, although I can feel the lethal vibrations as the animals are mowed down. When my eyes fully adjust to the night, I can all-too-vividly discern the carnage left on the road. Dozens of mangled bodies, many still fluttering in the final moments of life, form a grotesque scene. I shift my gaze skyward and do all I can to concentrate on the grimacing face in the full moon.

Phantasms in Dust

LAST NIGHT'S EXPERIENCE has left its imprint on us, and we are more determined than ever to get out of this place, so before seven o'clock we are out on the highway. However, it isn't long before our sense of hopelessness returns. What few cars there are at this hour pass us as though we were invisible.

"Maybe this spot is jinxed," said my father, and we move down the road a few hundred feet.

I regard this as a sign of commitment on his part to stay put until someone gives us a ride, and when he says this is the day our luck is going to change I believe him. But a few hours later when not a single car has so much as slowed down when it passes us, I remind myself that believing what he says is foolish business.

About the time the sun is nearly directly above us, the city in the mirage reappears in the desert lake, and upon close scrutiny I determine that it is different from yesterday's. The buildings and people are of another place.

A woman dashing down the street looks very familiar to me and when I say that I think it is my mother, my father says I am batty from the sun and that there is no way a reflection of Albany, New York, could reach this far. Still, I'm convinced of what I see and I strain my eyes to follow her thin figure until it melts into the pulsating trough that edges the scene. When she has evaporated I closely scan the street in the hope that she will reappear, but all I see are strangers.

My father has packed a small container of Bluebird grapefruit juice and two hard-boiled eggs into our canvas bag so that we don't have to return to the apartment until absolutely necessary. With a dollar and change from Gun he buys a couple of packs of Camels and a Hershey's bar, which is warm goo when he later removes it from his pants pocket.

We sit on a stone marker that is engraved with letters that don't form any word we know and have our lunch as a vulture circles overhead.

"It's just a crow," contends my father, but I have seen enough vultures in the movies to know the difference.

Later the vulture is joined by another and my father chucks a stone at the sky. The stone lands with a clank on the trailer portion of a passing truck, yet not even that gets us noticed.

As the afternoon deepens it seems we are doomed to return to our borrowed home back in Barstow, but in the middle of my father's gloomy rendition of Tony Bennett's hit song "Because of You," a tune I figure he associates with my mother, and my own umpteenth performance of "Be My Love," a car stops and offers us a ride to Las Vegas.

The Fun of Flames

MY FATHER HAS A JOB shilling at the Lucky Club. He pretends to be a customer to lure would-be gamblers to his blackjack table. It is a perfect job, he says, because you get paid for playing with the casino's money. When I ask if he can keep what he wins, he says only if you want to get your knuckles broken.

"No 'one for them and one for me' crap like at the carnival. You don't cheat these guys unless you want to play keno with the worms," he comments, talking like an old gambling pro.

It has been a week since we arrived and we have a small room with a hot plate compliments of our landlady, a Mrs. Carlisle, whose extraordinary height and waist-length auburn hair make her a unique vision to behold. I gauge her to be well over six feet because my father has to tilt his head slightly upward to speak with her. She is a recent widow, she says, and fortunately for us is very sympathetic to our well-rehearsed story about trying to raise money to send for my sick mother. This time she is plagued by chronic arthritis with a touch of asthma thrown in for good measure, and my father says he needs to get her to a dry climate like Nevada's in order for her to recuperate.

"The joints in her hands are always sore and swollen back east because it's so damp there. She's in a lot of pain and can't do much, not even the simple things like the dishes and laundry, which when there's three kids is a real problem," says my father in a way that lends considerable credence to his account of our predicament.

Mrs. Carlisle is totally won over by my father's melancholy soliloquy and says that he's a good man, a hero even, and that he deserves a lot of credit for fighting to keep his family together and single-handedly caring for a child. The irony of this statement does not escape me, but my father is lapping it up, saying that it is wonderful to have another understanding adult to talk to.

During the days I mostly hang out on Fremont Street, where all the downtown casinos are located. There is also a place called the Strip, which I never get to see. It is against the law for minors to enter the gambling establishments, so I watch the activity from the street.

Occasionally I catch sight of my father shilling, but he really can't acknowledge me because it might blow his cover, he says. He works the 3 to 11 P.M. shift, and I go to bed early to pass the time. When he gets his first paycheck we'll get a bus ticket as far as we can. There's no more discussion about my going back to Albany alone, and hitchhiking is out of the question again because the memory of the Mojave is still fresh in his mind.

He is intrigued by the extravagant gambling habits of a Chinese patron of the Lucky Club who plays the double silver-dollar slot machine.

"He drops a couple of grand or more into that damn machine. He must be loaded to do that practically every night like he does. Owns a laundry, I think, but everyone jokes that he's the one being taken to the cleaners. Nice guy, though. Last night he hit a jackpot for five thousand and ended up putting most of it back into the machine. He gave everybody a big tip too, except me. Shills are supposed to keep their identity secret, so he doesn't know I work for the club. The casino keeps the drinks coming, so he just sits on his stool and feeds the one-armed bandit."

I fantasize winning five thousand dollars. The first thing I would buy, I tell my father, is a train ticket back to Albany, since trains are fancier than buses, and passengers can walk around and eat while still moving toward their destination. Then I would give him, my mother, and my sisters a thousand dollars each. With my thousand I would buy a Columbia bicycle with whitewalls and maybe some snakeskin boots like Bo's. I might go to Florida too, I say, and my father comments that there are plenty of big hotels down there, especially in Miami Beach, where he could get a great bellhopping job during the season. I remind him that with the thousand bucks I just gave him he wouldn't have to work.

"Money doesn't last forever," he says, and I revise the amount in my fantasy upward to a hundred thousand dollars, a sum he agrees would do anyone for life.

As usual, used comic books are my main source of entertainment when I hang out in our room. A store nearby sells old comics three for a dime and trades three for any five you've read, so I spend my evenings with Archie, Donald, and Clark Kent. To my disappointment the store doesn't have any regular books, like *Robinson Crusoe* or *Winnie-the-Pooh*.

A large fire at a warehouse at the end of our street is well under way when my father comes home from work one night, so we go watch as dozens of firemen battle the blaze, which lights up the sky for miles. Fires are one of my father's favorite subjects and whenever he sees a fire truck or hears a siren he talks about a New York mayor who also was a fan of burning buildings.

"La Guardia chased fire trucks all over the city. He'd take off in the middle of a speech just to watch something burn down. He was a great mayor. Everybody loved him."

When a two-story wall crumbles to the ground, he cheers along with the crowd that has gathered and remarks that there is nothing quite like a good blaze to get the old heart pumping. We stay and watch until the flames are doused and there is nothing remaining but smoldering ash. By then we are among the few remaining spectators.

It is after two in the morning when we return to our stuffy box of a room and my father is too wound up to sleep. I can hardly keep my eyes open while he tells me about a fire that took down a house owned by a colored family in his old neighborhood when he was my age. He recounts the story as he runs the beam of his flashlight along the darkened ceiling and walls, and I think he probably wishes it were a flamethrower.

"My uncle Ed hated blackies, so we all figured that he struck the match himself. Maybe he did. Who knows? The house was right across the street from his. He was a funny guy. Always gave me a few bucks when I saw him. Used to say, 'Hey, Curt, make your first million yet?' Then he'd give me a handful of crumpled bills. He made his dough as a haberdasher down in the Garment District. Did okay too. Had a big Olds that he claimed the coons scratched up because they knew he hated their black asses."

I ask if he's still alive and my father says he's not sure. Lost touch with him decades ago, he explains. The last he heard, his uncle was living down in Florida because his old street had gone all colored.

"Some fire, eh?" he says, smothering the ray of his Eveready and sitting silently in the dark. I fall asleep keeping a wary eye on the glowing tip of his cigarette.

White Bread and Sugar

IT HITS NINETY-FIVE degrees and I overhear Mrs. Carlisle telling someone—apparently another newcomer to the area—that he'd better get used to it because when summer comes full-blown in Nevada it can melt granite. When I venture outside to test the mounting temperature, it doesn't feel as hot as I think it should. The sidewalks in the neighborhood are mostly deserted and there is less traffic than usual, or so it strikes me. The charred remains of the warehouse give the impression that it was the desert sun that brought it down.

Wandering past the scorched debris, I recall asking my teacher back in Albany if the Sun was capable of setting things on fire and being told that if Earth got any closer to the Sun than it already was, it would ignite like a bomb. Her answer kept me awake nights until I got the courage to ask if there was a chance that this would actually happen and was told that if anything, the opposite was more likely to occur. Her follow-up theory had the planet drifting out of its solar orbit, thus creating a new ice age and the global destruction of all living things. This gave me something new to worry about.

On Fremont Street I observe that the air-conditioning spilling out of the open-doored casinos gets about a third of the way across the sidewalk, so I limit my roving to within its refreshing reach. Mainly I station myself in front of my father's casino, where I catch sight of him at a poker table. His back is to me, so there is no way

I can make him aware of my presence. On the occasions he spots me, all he can do is wink or nod when the pit boss and dealer aren't watching him. We meet at the employees' entrance in back during his breaks, and then I usually return to our room and listen to my rocket radio and read or draw on the brown grocery bags I have discovered in the back hall.

My pirate sketch is as good as the one on the matchbook cover, says my father, so I contemplate becoming an artist until I remember how unhappy Kirk Douglas was in a movie about a famous painter who cuts off his ear. My father tells me that someone named Norman Corwin wrote the screenplay for that flick, adding that Corwin was a famous radio writer and director before TV came along and ruined everything. There's nothing like radio because it made you use your imagination, he remarks, complaining that TV is for idiots. He hates television, but I love and miss it and I'm no idiot, I protest.

"Yeah, well, that's because you don't get to watch it that much," he smugly replies, as if he has thoughtfully planned this for my own good.

The only thing there is to eat, besides a can of stewed tomatoes and a tin of sardines, is part of a loaf of white bread and some sugar. My father tells me to make some hobo stew by mixing a little of everything with the tomatoes, but I like bread-and-sugar sandwiches, so this becomes my meal as well as snack. When my father gets home he's upset because most of the bread is gone.

"You can't gobble up everything. I don't get paid for a while, you know, so we have to ration what we got," he complains, spreading a single sardine on a crust of bread with the back of his bent coffee spoon.

"Dinner is served!" I announce, but neither of us laughs as ultimately there is not much humor in starvation.

He is off the next day, so we stroll past the row of busy casinos and watch the tourists empty cups of silver into the slot machines. My father points out that the slots at a casino just up the street from his are reputed to be the most generous in town.

"More jackpots at the Golden Nugget than anywhere else, even out on the Strip," he says as we stand on the street and peer in. "Maybe I'll try a couple of nickels and see if I can hit one."

Although he is talking about the last of our change, I'm all for it. From my vantage point on the sidewalk I coach him on which machine to try, and he inserts a nickel and pulls the arm. A few coins drop from the machine and he returns with a wide grin to show me his winnings, which amount to fifty cents.

He hands me half of the bonanza and reenters the casino to see if he can find another hot machine. He is down to his last coin when the light on top of the slot lights up and a bell rings.

"Jackpot!" he shouts.

A Fool and His Money

A WRISTWATCH IS the first thing my father wants to purchase with part of the one-hundred-dollar winnings, but at my urging he defers that pleasure for the singular rewards of a decent meal. I calculate it will be our first legitimate feed since Lu Chow's, back in California. My goal is to devour something substantial and savory.

Our windfall will buy us tickets home, I remind my father, and he says that all I think about is hitting the road and moving on. He comments that I must have gypsy blood and then says that he knows I want to get back to my old lady and that jerk-burg place, Albany, but first he needs to relax. There is a remote and dreamy look in his eyes and I warn him not to start drinking now that he has so much money.

"You got a one-track mind, kiddo. For Christ's sake, I been working hard. There's more to shilling than just sitting around and playing cards, you know," he protests, and when I ask just what, he says never mind.

We'll catch a bus back tomorrow, so let's get off the subject, he says, and I propose we take in a movie. Maybe that's what we'll do, he responds, but before that he wants to see if the pawnshop around the corner from the Lucky Club has a quality timepiece, as he calls it. A Hamilton is what he's in the market for, and it is the brand he will sport haughtily, like some kind of tycoon, over the balance of his life—except when his watch is in hock somewhere.

"No Bulova or Longines. They're crap. Hamiltons are the best. My father swore by his, and his father too, and they could afford the finest."

We consider eating at one of the casino restaurants but then decide in favor of a small greasy spoon a few blocks off the center of town that advertises cheap homemade food on a large blackboard propped up in its window. I have passed the place many times and been tortured by the aromas of food pouring from its air vents.

My father has a ham-and-cheese sandwich and coffee. He is too distracted by the roll of $10.00 bills in his pocket to care much about eating. On the other hand I consume a plateful of chopped steak, smothered with onions, and mashed potatoes and wash it down with a butterscotch pudding. The check comes to $2.85, causing my father to arch his blackened eyebrow like Robert Taylor. He reluctantly doles out the sum to the cashier, leaving a quarter tip on our table, and we head to the pawnshop he knows about.

On the way I make note that a double feature starring Burt Lancaster and Guy Madison is playing at the theater near the casino district, but my father is not thrilled with their western themes because he has had enough of the West for a while. He says that maybe he'll just drop me off and go look for his watch while I'm at the movie. The ticket clerk says that I'll be out around six o'clock, and my father promises he'll be waiting for me.

"Have a good time, Butch. I'm just going to look around, maybe get a paper and sit in the shade somewhere. We'll go to the bus station when you get out, okay?" he says when I look at him skeptically and make him promise to behave himself.

The theater is dark and deliciously cool. I come in at the middle of the second feature when Guy Madison is duking it out with a saloonful of bad guys and take an aisle seat a few rows back from the screen. Not long after I settle in, I detect activity behind me. During the climactic gunfight scene I hear a rustle of clothing and heavy breathing and can feel pressure against the back of my seat, as if someone's knees are pressed against it.

When I get up to change seats I glance behind me and see a teenage boy and girl making out. I'm relieved that it isn't the kind of person I've encountered in other public places. For the rest of the movie I sit undisturbed in the very front row. A few hours later the saloon-fight scene returns and I depart the sanctuary of the movie house to find my father nowhere in sight.

Down the street there is a flashing neon sign with the familiar cocktail glass and bubbles rising from it and I decide to play my hunch and see if he is there. It takes my eyes a few seconds to adjust to the darkness of the interior as I peek in from the street, and I spot my father sitting at the bar talking with another patron. From just inside the entrance I whistle the signal we have devised in case we are separated or in danger and after a while I catch his attention. He acts thrilled to see me and I can tell that he is totally stewed.

"Mikey, come on over to your ole dad. I want you to meet my friend Roger," he blurts out, weaving like a top on his stool.

Roger is as drunk as my father and calls me "sport" after every sentence. "You're a pretty big little guy, aren't you, sport? You got a great old man here, sport. Did you know that, sport? Hey, you want a drink, sport? Not booze—I mean a soda or something, sport. Whaddya say, sport?"

Both sleeves of his denim work shirt are rolled up, revealing several tattoos with military themes. There are massive sweat stains under his arms and I figure the foul odor coming from him is responsible for the empty bar stools in his immediate vicinity. I tell him that we have to leave, but my father insists on having one more round, so I sit next to him while he orders another beer for both himself and his gamy chum.

"And give the midget a boilermaker," he jokes to the bartender, who says I'll have to sit at a table because it's against the law for minors to sit at the bar.

"He's thirty-nine, like Jack Benny. Just very short for his age," quips my father as I take a chair at a nearby table. "Hey, Butch, look what I got," he says, holding up his left arm. "It's a Hamilton, a real beauty, and I practically stole it. Nineteen bucks. You like it?"

Roger agrees that it's a beauty, better than his old pocket watch, and I try to calculate how much money he might have left. Sixty dollars maybe, and when he orders another round of drinks and one for the bartender I become infuriated.

"This is it," he promises, and by now he can hardly balance himself on the stool.

When Roger goes stumbling off in search of the men's room, I seize my father's arm and direct him out of the bar.

"Jesus, it's bright out here," he complains, attempting to hold his hand over his squinting eyes.

He is drunker than I estimated and I can barely keep him from toppling to the pavement.

"You're a good boy, Mikey-Bikey. You watch out for your old dad, don't you? No one else does, that's for sure. Not even when I was a kid your age. My old man didn't give a shit. Your mother has no use for me either. What does she do? Gets the cops after me," he moans, trying to extract a pack of cigarettes from his shirt pocket and failing.

Instead of returning to our room, I lead him to the bus station with the idea of making a break for it. Once we're there he all but passes out in his seat. There is less than forty dollars in his wallet and when I ask the ticket agent the fare to Albany I learn we don't have enough, even with me traveling half fare.

There is a large map of the United States on the wall behind the ticket windows, and I decide to purchase us passage to Fort Worth, Texas, a town a good distance away and with a name that appeals to me. A little after eight the bus is set to board and I guide my father to the departure gate. He is still so numb from the effects of the liquor that he is only vaguely aware that something is happening, and when I get him on the bus and in his seat, which is no small maneuver, he conks out instantly.

Before the bus departs, the driver comes back to us and asks if everything is all right. I say that my father is fine, just a little tired, and he remarks that my father smells like he stole the keys to the brewery.

"If he gets sick, get him to the john over there. I don't want him to heave all over everything. You never get that stink out of the bus," he says, and takes his place behind the wheel.

Across the narrow aisle a young woman cradling an infant eyes us with disapproval as the bus finally pulls out of the depot. Good-bye, Vegas. Hello, Texas, I say to myself as we travel past the seemingly endless row of fiery-bright gambling establishments and head out into the pitch-black Nevada desert that engulfs them. Inside the bus I feel content and secure. Sitting in a moving Greyhound is the closest I come to experiencing the bliss of home. If I could, I would live on one forever.

PART VI
LAS VEGAS TO FORT WORTH
(1,208 Miles)

Material Losses

"JESUS CHRIST, what about our stuff?" asks my father the next morning when he comes to, and I remind him that we have almost everything we own with us, except for his Gillette razor and our Denver thrift store coats, which we don't need because it is hot in Texas, and then I remember my rocket radio.

"And my flashlight. What about my flashlight?" he asks, nearly unhinged.

When the bus makes a stopover in Amarillo he wants to find a bar, but there is no fight left in him and a formidable amount remaining in me. At my greater insistence he sips some black coffee, and his hand shakes so much that I think he is going to dump it in his lap.

By the time the bus arrives in Fort Worth it is late in the day and my father is attempting to figure out our next move.

"Shit, of all the places to end up, and we don't even have our bag," he complains despairingly as the Greyhound passes the FORT WORTH CITY LIMITS sign. "How's it going to look without our luggage? They'll think we're goddamn bums, and no one will help us out."

He has a loud coughing fit and ultimately chucks the considerable accumulation of phlegm from his windpipe into a balled-up napkin that he has been clutching since the bar in Las Vegas. There is a brown stain above his shirt pocket, a drool mark, which all the rubbing in the world fails to remove. This compounds his blues.

When the bus pulls into its stall at the depot, it is like the lights going on when the movie is over.

A Dapper Friend

TEXAS CALLS ITSELF the Lone Star State and I can understand why. Not since we started out on the road have I experienced such awful loneliness. Most of the time I feel invisible because everyone around me seems to know or be recognized by somebody else. Their existences are confirmed by friends and family, yet I have no one to confirm mine except my father, who is as intangible to the world as I am.

We have another drably furnished light-housekeeping room in a large, quiet house about a mile from downtown. When we arrive my father finds us lodging through an ad in the newspaper, and again he is successful in getting the landlady to defer the rent payment until he can round up some employment. His winning strategy involves dealing only with women. Men, he says, don't buy a story as quickly or as easily. According to my mother, he is a great storyteller, especially when it comes to conning women out of something.

He is steadfastly opposed to hitting the road with our thumbs. Hitchhiking appears a dead issue. His distaste for thumbing has reached new heights since our episode in the desert, so he finds a job in the stockroom of a Woolworth dime store, which he says will give us enough dough to get home . . . a familiar promise.

For a while he considers calling my mother and putting the touch on her again, to use his words, but then he abandons the idea, saying that he can't deal with her ranting and raving. I think he still wants to keep our whereabouts secret so that she doesn't send the police after us. At the rate we're going, I tell him, it will take us years to get back.

"Why are you in such a big rush to get to a place you wanted to leave so bad? It's not that you loved it there. I shouldn't have let you talk me into going to California in the first place," he responds, and I say that it wasn't only my idea.

"Bullshit! You harped on it for more than a year. That's all I ever heard from you. 'Let's go to California. When can we go to California? I want to go to California,'" he says, mimicking me.

"I really didn't want to leave California. You got us kicked out," I shoot back, punching the palm of my hand threateningly.

My father scoffs at this symbolic display of anger.

"Oh, you're a real tough guy. I'm so afraid. Where's the flyswatter?" he taunts me, and when he isn't looking I thumb my nose at him.

There is not much to do or see in Fort Worth, I conclude after wandering around the city for several days, so I mostly hang out at the house, either on the front steps or in our room.

Whoever else lives in the house is never around, so there is no one to talk to the way there was at the Encino Paradise Motel or at Pearl's place in Indianapolis. When my father gets back from work he is too pooped-out from moving merchandise to be very good company.

"Damn place kills my back," he complains.

"Then let's just go. We can get a ride," I pitch, but he says we're better off here until he can get enough dough to get the bus and replace our canvas bag.

"No one is going to pick us up without our luggage. They'll think something is wrong, that I'm kidnapping you. It just won't look right that we're trying to get back east and we don't have anything with us. If we're stopped by the cops out on the road, what are we going to say without a suitcase? Nobody respectable travels that way."

"We can say it was stolen," I offer, but my father tells me to for-get it—we're staying and that's that.

Late one morning there is a knock on the door as I am in the middle of writing a story about a cowboy who gets his superhuman strength from kryptonite, the very substance that drains Superman of his powers. I think it is probably the landlady inquiring about the rent, but it turns out to be a slender man with wispy strands of blond hair that stick out over his black-rimmed glasses. He intro-duces himself as Ryan, our neighbor.

"I live down the hall. I saw you and your father a couple of times, but you guys didn't see me. Is your father here?" he asks, looking past me into our room.

He's at work, I tell him, and he says he wanted to know if we'd like to have lunch with him in his place. Says he's made some pea soup, an old family recipe, and would be glad to share it with us.

"Well, you're welcome to have a bowl with me," he says, and al-though pea soup doesn't sound all that tasty to me, the idea of com-pany does, and besides, Ryan seems okay.

His room is twice the size of ours and he has a kitchenette con-cealed behind some plastic curtains. Everything is very neat and clean and the walls are covered with floral paintings that brighten the room and make it all the more inviting to me. His furniture is covered in flower patterns as well. A double bed is located in the very center of the room and is decorated with pillows and a white spread with the kind of fuzzy stitching that reminds me of my mother's robe. When I tell him this, he reports that it's a fabric called chenille.

"It's a beautiful room," I tell Ryan, and he is very pleased.

"Are you from Fort Worth?" he asks while carefully ladling thick green liquid into a bowl set on a yellow-and-black-checkered table-cloth.

"Have a seat," he says, pulling one out for me, and I give him the party line on my father and me, incorporating a few new variations into the tale.

"So your father got a job? Doing what?" he asks as I sample the soup, which is much better than I expected.

"He's a stock clerk at Woolworth but he actually works in the hotel racket," I answer, employing my father's term for his profession.

"Do you like the soup? My mother made it for me every Thursday when I was growing up. At least you have both your parents, even if your mother does have amnesia. I lost my father in the war. He died fighting in the South Pacific, so it was just me and Mother. I have his medal, a Purple Heart. Would you like to see it?"

He removes a small black velvet box from the bottom drawer of a dresser that also contains several shirts wrapped in paper bands with cardboard in their collars. He asks if I'm ready and then he unveils the medal slowly and ceremoniously.

"I love the color. Don't you? It's somehow just right for the reason they award it. Like a bruise or a wound. My father was very brave, my mother said. He led a charge up a hill occupied by Japs. Did you ever see *To Hell and Back*? It's about Audie Murphy, the war hero and actor. He reminds me of my father. Very courageous. Would you like to put it on?"

Sure, I say, and stand in front of a mirror imagining that it is my father's long-lost medal for his jeep injury and that he has given it to me to display his heroism to the world.

"I'm off work tomorrow. Actually, I'm on vacation this week. The funeral home where I work is closed."

I ask what he does at the funeral home and he says that he's an embalmer's assistant, which means he does a little bit of everything.

"I help out with the clients and sometimes drive the limousine or hearse."

"Clients?" I ask, sensing that he is talking about dead people, and he confirms my suspicion.

"We call them clients because that's what they actually are, only they can't talk back," he says with a funny chuckle. "How'd you like to see where I work? It's very nice."

This I'm not sure about, but I'm drawn enough by morbid curiosity and a desire for companionship to accept his invitation.

"Wonderful. How about ten o'clock, or do you sleep late?" he asks, and I tell him that I'm up at sunrise.

"Not me. I love to sack in, especially on holiday. That's what they call it in England, you know. Not vacation, but holiday," he says, using an accent that makes him sound like David Niven. "So much classier-sounding, I think. Anyway, I never sleep past nine o'clock, even when I'm on holiday," he adds, taking a birdlike sip of his soup and calling it yummy.

When I finish eating he asks if I'd like to go for a walk, but I say that I'm meeting my father at his work, even though it is two hours before he gets out.

"Well, then, I'll see you in the morning," he says, and extends his hand for me to shake.

His grip is soft and prolonged, so I take the opportunity to demonstrate my physical prowess and squeeze his hand with all of my might.

"My lord, don't break it," he says with a melodramatic flare, and I apologize for not knowing my own strength. "Yes, you certainly are a strong one. It still works, I think. You're what is called wiry. Strong even if you are slight in build. I'm slight in build but not very strong, so I guess that makes me wireless. Ha! That's what the British call their radio. Did you know that?"

No, I say, and he says not to pay any attention to him because he just gets the jabbers sometimes and doesn't know when to stop. Later on my walk to meet my father, the two things that stand out in my mind most about Ryan are his aftershave lotion, which reminds me of burning logs, and the crisp white T-shirt visible under the collar of his starched pale yellow sport shirt.

After months on the road my only remaining undershirt is worn and discolored beyond redemption, so I decide to take immediate action to rectify this and remove it in an alley. Later when I get a chance to check myself out in a mirror, I am pleased with the improvement this makes and so I do the same with my ravaged undershorts, which lately my nose has begun to detect.

"Jesus Christ, even dirty underwear is better than none!" is my father's reaction to the measures I have taken to look and smell as good as Ryan.

Not Hoppy

RED SKELTON'S SON is dying of leukemia, just like the Scanlons' girl in New York, and I think I am too. I have pains in my fingers like Tyrone Power in *The Eddy Duchin Story*. My father says it's all in my head, but every time I think of the pianist's contorted hands on the keyboard it seems very real to me.

"Red Skelton took his son to see the pope," I report, having seen this in the newspaper section that lists current movies and television programs.

He asks why and I tell him about the comedian's cancer-stricken little boy.

"That's too bad, but that's not going to help much. Once you get cancer you might as well write your will," he says, and I tell him that it has to do with the white cells eating the red cells, or maybe the other way around.

"Who told you about this?" he asks, and I tell him that it was in the same newspaper article about Red Skelton's son.

"And you think that's what you got? Well, I'll call the Vatican and make you an appointment with the pope too. Maybe you and Red's son can become best friends, since you share so much in common," he teases, but I am not amused, especially since I can feel the white cells gobbling up the red ones in my knuckles and joints at the very moment.

We are walking home and pass the pawnshop where my father's

Hamilton is being kept until he can come up with the $5.50 to get it out of hock.

"I always feel naked without a timepiece," he laments as we peer through the window at several rows of pawned watches. "Mostly Bulovas. Probably only gave a couple of bucks for them. They keep okay time, but not like a Hamilton."

There is a bugle on display for $5.00, and I tell my father that I think I could learn to play well enough to get a job in a band in no time, to which he replies that I don't have the right kind of choppers to play wind instruments.

"When I sang on the radio at the Bond Hotel I hung out with some musicians. Learned a few tricks of the trade. Back then I had decent teeth of my own and was thinking about playing the horn too—not the bugle but the trumpet—but I had the same problem as you. Your front teeth slant inward. To play the trumpet or bugle you got to have teeth that slant out. If you don't, they loosen and fall out. You don't see too many toothless horn players."

"What about ones with false teeth?" I ask, attempting to get his goat, and then I argue that my teeth don't go in that much and that they are very strong.

"Look," I say, sticking my mouth open at him and inviting him to test them.

He takes my front teeth between his fingers and refuses to let go.

"Say 'Please with jelly on it,'" he teases, and I try to twist free. "Now you got to say 'Please with jelly and raisins on it.' Then I'll let you go."

When I try to talk, he laughs and remarks that I sound like Elmer Fudd, so I jab him in the arm and break his hold.

"What the hell's the matter with you! I have bursitis, you little dope," he complains, rubbing his arm and continuing to fume.

I ask him what bursitis is and he says it's something you get from lifting and carrying heavy objects, like suitcases at the DeWitt Clinton Hotel and boxes at Woolworth, so that he can support me. He is peeved by my assault and for several minutes we say nothing as we continue our walk home. About a block away from our rooming house I tell him about Ryan and he says I shouldn't be too quick to chum up with strangers.

"There's a lot of creeps around," he warns, and when I tell him that Ryan works in a funeral parlor, he says that's all the more reason to be wary of him.

At the variety store a few doors down from the rooming house, we purchase something for supper. As we're standing at the cash register I spot Ryan moving by on the other side of the street. He is carrying an umbrella even though it is sunny and there has not been any rain or clouds in Fort Worth since we arrived. By the time I get my father to look at him, Ryan has disappeared around the corner.

"Maybe he has a date with one of his clients," my father remarks as the cashier tells him what he owes for a can of hash, a loaf of bread, a pint of milk, and a Sky Bar.

The climb up to our room triggers a coughing spell in my father that only abates when he has heaved up a giant glob of phlegm into our tin trash basket. When I lodge my disgust, my father says to shut up or he'll use my pillow the next time. It's all his smoking, I tell him, and he says it's bronchitis and that he's had it since he was a kid. I think at least it doesn't kill people, like leukemia.

"So are you going to eat that candy bar or just look at it?" he asks, trying to suppress another respiratory spasm and sounding like the old London air-raid siren.

Whenever he refers this way to any candy I might have, I know he is really asking for some, although he is not a big sweet-eater, he claims. Before he pops the small piece I have given him into his mouth, he removes his false teeth, and a long string of yellow drool swings from it as he places it on the dresser. When I complain that this makes me lose my appetite, he says that's good and to give him the rest of my candy bar, which I refuse to do.

After supper we kill the evening by strolling back downtown. In a department store a small crowd has gathered around someone a poster promotes as Tex Ritter, who is handing out autographed photos of himself. He is dressed like a cowboy and we learn that he is a popular country-and-western singer.

"Not exactly Hopalong Cassidy," remarks my father, inspecting the black-and-white glossy as we drift through the twilight streets of the North Texas city.

Before the sun reaches the horizon it is absorbed by a thick brown haze that I notice has been reaching higher in the western sky each day. When I mention this my father comments that it's a good thing we're heading east because it looks like the entire West is turning into a big wall of shit.

The Dearly Departed

RYAN IS WAITING in the hall with his umbrella. It is a few minutes before ten and it occurs to me that he may have been standing outside the door for a while. Although it is already very warm, he is wearing a black sport jacket with gold buttons and a small gray hat—a beret, he calls it—that makes him look like a foreigner. I have on my threadbare pants and a new fifty-nine-cent T-shirt that I demanded my father buy me at a downtown army surplus store. When he paid for it out of the five-dollar advance he'd received from work, he complained that he hadn't bought himself anything new since we left Albany, and I reminded him that he had just purchased a new Maybelline eyebrow pencil. This made him hot under the collar and he threatened to spend the balance of his paycheck when he got it to upgrade his wardrobe, stating that his slacks were so worn you could see yourself in them. Forget a bus ticket, he bellowed, adding that he was tired of looking like a bum and that people judge you by your appearance.

"Morning, Master Keith," says Ryan when I emerge from our room.

He has a large grin on his smooth, whiskerless face. For the first time I notice that his teeth are very white and even, like John Kennedy's, and I wonder if they are actually his.

"Is there something on my face?" he asks, catching my stare, and I tell him that he has real nice teeth.

"Thank you. My Auntie Doris insisted on annual visits to the dentist. She was a big help to my mother and me after my father died. I wore braces for three years, you know. It was a pain, especially what the other kids said, but I like how they turned out, so I shouldn't complain. You seem to have good teeth too," he remarks, focusing his eyes on my mouth, and I tell him that I've only been to the dentist one time and that single visit resulted in two back teeth being pulled.

When I probe the left side of my mouth with my tongue I can feel a large hole developing in one of my existing teeth, and sometimes when I chew with it, it's painful. I withhold this information from him so as not to diminish his opinion.

"Brushing is the key. After every meal too, not just at bedtime. I use Ipana, like Bucky Beaver. 'Brusha, brusha, brusha.' "

He sings the TV jingle and smiles widely so that I can behold his perfect teeth again. Since my toothbrush was also one of the things left behind in Las Vegas, oral hygiene has not been a major concern, not that it ever was.

On the way to the funeral home I ask Ryan why he always carries his umbrella and he says for protection.

"A few months ago, on my way home from work, a couple of punks robbed me, and one of them had a switchblade."

"Was it a stiletto?" I ask, and he says he has no idea.

"Is that some kind of knife?" he inquires, and I tell him about Joey Ramone back in Denver, saying nothing about our scrape with the law lest he think we too were punks.

"Anyway, I decided that I need to protect myself, so I bought this umbrella. It's a very good one, sturdy, and I sharpened the metal tip. If those bloody blokes try something again, they're in for a big surprise."

To demonstrate his intent he spears a piece of paper on the ground and hands it to me.

"Go ahead, feel the tip. Careful though—it'll pierce armor. I don't care if I kill those kids, really. Do you know what else they did to me? They made me kneel down and they urinated on me. Imagine that!

I think God was getting back at me for doing the same thing to my Aunt Doris's blind sister-in-law when I was little. Poor woman. It makes me want to cry to think about it now. She was an invalid in a wheelchair, and one time when we visited her and my two other old aunts, I peed right in her lap when we were alone. She didn't know what was going on. Thought she was on the porch by herself. Later everybody just figured that she wet herself. To this day I don't know why I did such a horrible thing. We all have a dark side, I guess. You're the first person I ever told that to, so please don't repeat it."

While we're walking along, Ryan treats his weapon as a cane and I advise him that hitting it on the pavement will dull the tip. He calls this a very astute observation and thanks me for making it, but a couple of moments later he is tapping away again.

"You know, those boys kept saying they were going to cut off my agates, and I thought they really meant it too," he says, rolling his eyes and frowning. "I think they would have if a car hadn't driven by. It scared them off, but they got my wallet and I thought they'd come looking for me because they had my address. Finally the police picked them up and I identified them in a lineup. They were sent to jail for six months, but they're due for release and I think they're going to come after me."

When two figures appear a couple of blocks ahead of us, Ryan insists that we hide inside a doorway just in case it is them. We remain completely still in the shadows until they pass. Fortunately they are not his attackers.

"I guess I didn't inherit my father's courage," he says, letting go of my hand after clutching it with considerably more force than he exerted in his handshake. "Maybe I'll get a pistol. One of those little derringers. Something you can tuck out of sight. I'm just not that strong physically."

I offer to teach him some boxing moves that I learned from the movies, but he says that a gun is probably the best way for him to go.

"At least the deceased can't hurt you," he comments as we approach the funeral home where he works.

Suddenly I have second thoughts about going inside, but Ryan assures me that in all the time he has worked as an undertaker's assistant he has never been attacked or pissed on by a corpse.

"Actually, people are much nicer when they're dead. No malice, no pettiness, no big egos. Nothing but the best virtues remain. Besides, the place is closed for vacation, so there's no clients here right now."

As we climb the few steps leading to the door of what looks to me like a beautiful mansion, a large cloud covers the sun, casting a dark, ominous shadow over everything. This is no coincidence as far as I'm concerned. It is a clear admonition from beyond and as Ryan opens the door I fully expect to be greeted by the living dead.

Tiny Pink Flowers

"THIS IS THE embalming room. It's where the clients are prepared for display and interment. We don't cremate here," comments Ryan as we stand beside the metal table upon which dead people are placed.

Inside a glass cabinet there are several large bottles and many are labeled with skulls and crossbones.

"That's embalming fluid and stuff. We drain all the blood and waste from the corpses and replace it with preservatives and disinfectant chemicals. Dead bodies can be very nasty, especially after rigor mortis sets in."

I ask what that is and am told that after a few hours a corpse stiffens because its muscle protein coagulates.

"Everything just hardens up. That's why they call a dead person a stiff. You can stand a body on its head in the corner after a few hours. It's better to get them while they're still fresh. I mean recently deceased. They're a little easier to prep. Of course, sometimes you can set their expressions easier when they reach the riggo stage. These are drain canals here on the side of the table and underneath is where we put a bucket to collect all the liquids and waste material. The table rises up at one end so that everything will just drain out," says Ryan, running his delicate fingers along the shiny platform.

The whole thing is giving me a giant case of the creeps and I gauge the distance to the door in case I want to make a quick escape.

"Sometimes we get clients who are already dried out or desiccated, as we call it—usually accident victims who have gaping wounds and have bled to death or cadavers that have been autopsied. That's when a coroner or doctor cuts them all up to find out the cause of death. One time a client came in without his head. He went under a truck like Jayne Mansfield did, only he was on a motorcycle. They never found his skull. Can you imagine that? When that kind of thing happens there is a closed-coffin service, so all we really do is pump them up with formaldehyde and stuff their hollow areas with cotton to meet state regs. There's no need for cosmetology either."

This is what makes dead people look like they did when they were alive, Ryan says, adding that in some cases the clients actually end up looking better as corpses.

"I do the hair sometimes, because I seem to have a flair for it. Mainly I wash and comb it, and I've started doing female hair lately. It's more difficult because it's longer and more styled usually. I did this young girl's last week. It wasn't easy because part of her forehead was crushed and a lot of her scalp had come off, but when I was through you couldn't tell the difference. She was so pretty and not much older than you, only fifteen. She was killed when a swing her little sister was on hit her in the head. Can you imagine that happening to anyone? She got too close when she was pushing it and wham! A real freak accident," he says, dramatizing his words by slapping the top of his head, causing his hat to fly off.

I am seconds away from calling it quits and bolting for the door.

"She had the cutest little figure. Just developing, you know. We had to prepare her for the embalmer, me and Daren. He works with me. Her skin was like a peach, so smooth and delicate. She had on these white panties with tiny pink flowers. Promise you won't tell anybody, but I think Daren humped her, because she was real fresh and even still warm down there," he says, pointing in the direction of his crotch.

"She was brought in real soon after the accident. Her parents didn't want an autopsy. Anyway, when I came back into the room after being away for about five minutes, he—I mean Daren—was acting peculiar, out of breath and sweaty, and I noticed something on her stomach that wasn't there before. I pretended not to see it. Listen, don't tell your dad that I told you this. I could get into trouble."

I promise not to repeat a word of what he has confided, and I wonder if it is all just a figment of his imagination, something he is making up to see how I'll react.

"Would you like to see a dead body sometime? Most people never have, you know, at least not before it's placed in a casket. Maybe next week or the week after, I can bring you over when nobody's here, just the client."

That would be great, I say, not meaning it, and he shows me the rest of the funeral home, which is not as interesting or scary as where we have just been. When the tour is over we go to a nearby restaurant and Ryan buys me a hot dog and soda.

We sit in a booth that overlooks a busy street. I happily finish Ryan's tuna sandwich at his request and order another soda. For several minutes neither of us speaks. He is lost in thought and when he finally says something there is a profoundly sad look in his eyes.

"Her name was Cindy. The girl that got killed by the swing, I mean. We had to clean her up, get the blood off and stuff. I could tell when we washed her that something funny had happened. There was sticky stuff in her private hairs. You know, near her pussy. I think it was come. She was so beautiful. You would have thought so too."

There is another stretch of silence and then he asks if I'd like to have supper with him tomorrow night.

"You can bring your father, okay?" he says, more as an afterthought.

On the way out of the restaurant Ryan believes he sees the punks who attacked him, so we remain in the entranceway with him holding on to me for dear life until he is certain otherwise.

"No, that's not them. This is really no way to live." He sighs, holding his weapon at the ready.

I sense that he is on the verge of tears but then he raises his umbrella high above his head and shouts, "Don't mess with Audie Murphy!"

Ryan Exposed

MY FATHER RELUCTANTLY agrees to have supper with Ryan, but when I knock on his door late in the day there is no answer. By six-thirty we've given up any hope of a free meal and eat some beans and canned potatoes, which seem particularly tasteless in my disappointed state of mind.

"Not a very reliable friend you got there, Butch," chides my father, who isn't all that unhappy by the no-show.

Later I tap on Ryan's door again but he is still not home. This makes me wonder if he has finally met up with his attackers, and I recount the story to my father. When I suggest that we go out and check the streets and alleys, my father says that I have an overactive imagination, and besides, he's not about to get involved in somebody else's problems because he has enough of his own.

"I'm sure he's fine. Probably just forgot, or maybe you didn't hear him right."

Around ten o'clock I hear footsteps in the hall and assume it is Ryan, but I don't check. I am perturbed and hurt that he would have forgotten about us and I resolve to avoid him in the future as a way of getting even.

"He's kind of weird," I admit to my father without going into any detail, and he says that I should choose my friends better.

"Who knows what his story is. Could be a real wacko. Besides, he's a grown-up. Find someone your own age to hang out with, but no little jerks with knives . . . I mean *stilettos,*" remarks my father tauntingly, and I ask him where, noting that it's not easy to meet kids when you don't go to school.

That night I dream about the girl who was hit in the head by the swing. She is pushing me rather than her little sister, and she is nude except for her white panties with pink flowers. She is as pretty as Ryan described but she has no breasts or nipples.

Do you want to go higher? she asks in a voice that is sweet and reminiscent of my sister Pamela's, and I answer, Yes . . . higher, much higher.

At one point the swing is so far in the sky that I wonder if it will make a complete loop, and when I look down I see that the girl is directly under me and in my path. As the swing descends I scream for her to get out of the way and I brace myself for the awful collision, but none occurs. When I open my eyes she is standing in the sandbox with Ryan, and they are both looking at me eerily. As the swing loses its altitude they glide across the ground toward me without moving their bodies, and I notice that the tip of Ryan's umbrella is inserted in the dead girl's bloodless foot and that two small gray twigs with tiny purple blossoms the color of Ryan's father's war medal are extended from her blank chest.

In the morning this image is vivid and unsettling to me, and after my father heads for work at Woolworth I visit the local playground, half expecting and fearing that I will encounter the dead girl there. It is empty, however, so I return to our room and reread some old comics. Shortly after ten o'clock there is a knock on the door and I know it is Ryan.

"Sorry I couldn't take you to supper, but my auntie Doris demanded my presence and I had to go over to Dallas. She gets into these moods and wants me to be with her. Would you like a cup of tea? I'm boiling water. It's Earl Grey. Real British tea."

When we're in Ryan's room he removes a photo album from a closet and shows me pictures of him and his mother and aunt from the time he was a baby. In every picture, until he is almost fully grown, he is dressed in short pants and suspenders. At twelve, in his braces, glasses, and shorts, he looks like the kind of kid everyone would pick on in school. A perfect target for pubescent hostilities.

"How about a corn muffin, Michael? They're homemade. Auntie Doris is a great confectioner. Used to be her trade, so when she's got the gloomies she cooks up a storm. My God, the house is simply bulging with baked goods."

Corn muffins sound only marginally appealing to me, but as usual I'm not about to refuse food. Ryan removes two muffins from a flowery container and places one before me.

"Those little orange specs are peels. Auntie puts them in to add some flavor. Here, put some real butter on them. I hate margarine. Don't you?"

Like the pea soup, the corn muffin tastes much better than I expect and when I'm done Ryan offers me another, but I decline since they seem such a treasure to him. Meanwhile he has barely made a dent in his muffin with his canary-like bites.

"Would you like to see some nasty photographs?" he asks, setting his nibbled muffin aside and removing an envelope from the back of his photo album, and I think of Web from Denver.

"Well, they're not really all that nasty, I suppose. Did you ever see a girl without clothes on?" he inquires while sorting through the envelope, and I wonder if he is going to show me a picture of his young client, who I just dreamed had twigs sprouting from her naked body.

I say that I have, again thinking back to the nudie magazine in Denver, but instead of telling him about it I recount the time I saw my sister's friend without her dress on.

"Were you playing doctor?" he asks enthusiastically after I tell him about being with Belinda La Pierre under the railroad trestle back in Albany.

"Did you go completely naked?" he asks with mounting interest, and I report that I wouldn't remove my underpants even though she wanted me to.

This heightens his excitement and he relates a similar story about a girl he knew in the third grade.

"She kept showing me her bush but wouldn't let me see anything else. I really wanted to see titties and heinie. Take a look at these," he says, handing me several photos of young kids, mostly boys, in their underwear.

"I took some of them. I have this camera that develops pictures in a minute. A Polaroid. Maybe I could take your picture."

He removes a camera from a case under his bed and aims it at me.

"'Hold it, I think you're going to like this one,'" he says, claiming to be quoting from the opening of *The Bob Cummings Show* on television.

"Do you remember that program?" he inquires, and I say kind of.

There is a flash of light and he promises that in a few moments I'll have something to send to Hollywood. When the picture has fully developed he hands it to me, remarking that I remind him of the kid on another television show called *The Rifleman*.

"Crawford, I think his name is," says Ryan, probing his memory, "but I can't recall his first name."

Others have told me that, I admit, thinking of Leland back at the Oxford Arms in New York.

"He did that awfully sweet song too. Such a charming little voice. Didn't you love it? Now let me get a full shot. Stand over there by the door, okay?"

After a couple more photos—beefcake, he calls them—Ryan asks if I'd like to have a picture to send to Belinda, something sexy, he says, and I tell him that I'm not really friends with her anymore.

"That's okay—you can give it to somebody else. Why don't you slip off your pants, or just lower them? I'll just take one picture and you can have it."

This suggestion riles me but I conceal my growing disdain. No more Web encounters for me, I have pledged, and so I make up an excuse about having to meet my father. Ryan's disappointment is

apparent but dissipates somewhat when I suggest that we do it another time. Yet he still pushes the idea of shooting the photo, saying that it will only take a moment and that I'll have a wonderful
picture to give to my next girlfriend. When I open the door to leave
he concedes that maybe another time would be better, and I sense
that he fears exposure.

"You like the movies, right? Would you like to go to a matinee
sometime?" he asks. "Here, take these pictures of you and send them
to your sisters. Bet they'd love to have photos of their good-looking
brother."

Back in my room I examine the snapshots and arrive at the de-
pressing conclusion that all I really look like is a dopey kid with too
much hair for such a skinny body—a human palm tree.

Storms and Debates

ON THE SUNDAY that I'm supposed to take in a matinee of *Rio Bravo* with Ryan, there is a dust storm. In the morning the sky is a dull brown and by midafternoon a huge wall of prairie dust is closing in on the city from the Texas Panhandle. From our room we watch nervously as the horizon darkens.

Our landlady has instructed us to close everything and she gives us rags to stuff into the cracks around the window in our room. There is a thin coat of dust everywhere already, and she says that when it's all over we'll be shoveling out.

"Y'all better cover your nose and mouth, 'cause it can clog you up pretty bad. Could end up with a lung disease like those coal miners get. Can catch pneumonia too. Some folks wrap their head in wet towels till it runs its course. No matter, you're gonna be covered with dust whatever you do, and when this passes you'll be spitting up Cream of Wheat. Just don't go outside. You can't see the hand in front of your nose when it's full-blown. Not that anybody in their right head would venture out."

She lends my father an old wooden Philco radio because he wants to listen to the presidential debates between Nixon and Kennedy later in the day. He can also keep track of the storm, she says, although she figures it will be long over before those two politicians start dueling. We can hear her give her dust storm speech to another tenant down the hall as the wind and sand begin to whip against the house with such force and racket that we wonder if we're safe inside. We turn the mattress on its side and wait out the storm behind it. At the storm's height it is as dark as night and I can feel the sand gathering on everything I touch. My father is nervous but I feel more excited than afraid as I try to imagine what it will look like when all the dust has fallen.

"Maybe it will be like after an atomic bomb is dropped," I speculate aloud, and my father just mumbles something about what a dump Texas is and that the Commies wouldn't waste their shit on such a hole as he strikes a match to light a cig.

In a couple of hours the wind dies down and it begins to brighten. The storm has passed and we've survived, but we both look several shades darker than we started out, as if we have spent the day at the beach or back on Route 66 in the California desert. The room is completely coated with dust as well and my father complains that our clothes are probably ruined. When I suggest that we just wash them, he says that we would never get the sand out, so there's no sense in even bothering. I disagree, saying that I plan to scrub my new T-shirt until I restore its former luster. Later when I remove it there is an outline of the storm on my body, and my father says that I don't need to wash my T-shirt because it looks like I'm already wearing one.

It is evening before we head out into the aftermath of the dirt blizzard to shake some of the accumulation from our bedcovers and clothes. We join several other people who are already doing the same in front of their houses, and this creates a mini dust storm of its own. The rising clouds form a halo around the streetlamps, and I'm intrigued by this spooky effect.

"What if it's really the end of the world?" I ask, caught up in the bizarre scene, and he remarks that at least that would mean the end of Tex-*ass,* placing special emphasis on the last syllable of the word.

The landlady overhears his comment and reacts as if she has been personally insulted. Picking up on this, my father says he's only joking and that in fact he's actually thinking of ways to get my afflicted mother and sisters out here sooner than he planned so that we can all get settled in the lovely city of Fort Worth. She is only mildly placated by his oratory and reminds him that we're behind in our rent.

Despite the day's events my father's mood is buoyed by Nixon's performance against Kennedy on the radio.

"He sure kicked that harp's fanny," he reports with a satisfied grin on his grimy face.

When we're in bed it feels like we're lying on a dirt road, and this renews my father's contempt for the nation's biggest dust bowl, as he calls it.

"Jesus, I'll be glad as hell when this place is only a bad memory," he grumbles, leaping out of the bed and brushing his half-naked body as if it were covered with fire ants.

Two days after the dust storm, I spot Ryan coming out of the building with a large suitcase. He says that he is going to stay with his aunt for a while for two reasons. One is to be with her because she is so lonely and depressed, and the other is to avoid running into the guys who robbed and peed on him. He claims he has seen them and figures that if they think he's no longer around they'll find someone else to abuse.

"Watch out for yourself. They're mean and don't care who they bother, and maybe they've seen you with me," he warns, waving his umbrella as he makes his getaway.

Until we board a bus a couple of months later, I maintain a constant vigil for Ryan's ruffians and with great relief never encounter anyone who even remotely matches their description.

PART VII
FORT WORTH TO ALBANY
(1,678 Miles)

East by Northeast

WE WILL ARRIVE in Cincinnati, Ohio, in early autumn on the exact date of my mother's birthday, so on the bus ride from Texas I make her a card. It is a drawing on a napkin of me in a jet fighter. In the airstream behind the plane I have printed the words "Happy Birthday, Mom." Beneath it I sketch the skyline of the city as I imagine it. I copy the spelling from our ticket stubs and write "Cincinnati or Bust" in the space between the building tops and the jet.

Entering the deserted city streets after two in the morning, we decide to pass the balance of the night on a bench in the empty bus station. There's no sense paying for a hotel room when there's only a few hours remaining before daylight, reasons my father.

As day breaks, my father studies the newspaper classifieds to get an idea where the largest concentration of rooming houses is located. Since there is no sign of a Travelers Aid anywhere, we seek directions to the area from a luggage clerk and we head out in search of our next residence.

The first house with a ROOM FOR RENT sign is practically collapsing from neglect but that doesn't deter my father, who rings the bell. When a heavy black woman holding a naked child answers, he pretends to be lost and asks directions to a street that is actually in Albany.

"What a dump," he comments as we move away.

The next house advertising rooms is in better repair but halfway through my father's patented speech the landlord all but pushes us out of the entranceway. This sends my father's mood plummeting, and when I say that we might as well just hit the road because we're never going to get a place to stay, he unleashes a barrage of odious observations about the people of Cincinnati.

Two more tries for lodging yield similar results, and he is about to check the phone book for the Salvation Army and homeless shelters when we spot a FOR RENT sign in the bay window of a gray-shingled three-story building. It is here that we land a place to lay our heads, and this is accomplished without even using the elaborate version of our sick-wife-and-mother story. My father simply states that money is on the way and indicates that he has a job lined up at the Sheraton Gibson Hotel, which we passed on our excursion to the low-rent district. I figure he gives the abbreviated text because he senses that the woman who owns the house is an easy touch. From the moment we inquire about the vacancy she never stops gabbing and giggling, and when my father raises the issue of our being a little short on cash and only able to pay for part of the week, she tells him not to worry about it and to pay her when he can. Cincinnati is not such a horrible place, concedes my father afterward.

There is a small beauty shop called Sheila's Coiffures on the first floor of the house. It turns out to be our new landlady's business, and I think it must be great having your name written in neon. All during our conversation she fiddles with her hair. A wig, my father tells me later, and he also comments on the size of her nose, saying it would give W. C. Fields an inferiority complex.

"You could park cars in that snout," he says, laughing harder than he has in a long time, and I tell him that is not a very nice thing to say about such a kind person, adding that he is just pleased to have found someone with a nose almost as big as his.

"Almost!" he shoots back. "My God, you need glasses, you little fart!"

We're given a room on the floor above the salon, overlooking a patio and a pleasant backyard. The first thing that catches my eye is a large black dog sprawled out on a collapsed lounge chair. I whistle to attract its attention and it looks up at me with only mild interest.

We have a small pantry that contains a hot plate and tiny icebox but no sink to serve as our nocturnal urinal. The toilet is down the hall. When I return from relieving myself my father tells me to look out the window. There are now several large dogs romping around in the backyard, and one is a beautiful collie that reminds me of Lassie.

"What the hell has she got down there, a kennel?" he remarks while discovering he is out of smokes. "Shit! Go ask Sheila where the nearest grocery story is and we'll get some grub."

When I tap on her apartment door there is a loud chorus of barking and growling. After a moment I hear her telling the dogs to quiet down. She refers to them by an odd assortment of names— Bascomb, Zeus, Raoul—and tells them to be good little guys for Mommy. She asks who is at the door and I reveal my identity and after a couple of seconds the door is opened a crack.

"I don't want them to get out," she says, and I'm thankful for that. "That's Wayland," she says when the nose of the collie sticks through the opening. "He's named after a fellow I had a crush on in high school. He's a real sweetie pie, this one. What can I do for you, hon?"

The closest grocery store is five blocks away, and Sheila says that as long as we're going there it would be helpful if we could pick up a ten-pound bag of dog food. She hands me the money through the crack in the door and I return to our room. My father is not thrilled at the prospect of lugging back dog chow.

"Shit! You should have said something about my back. Ten pounds is a lot to carry that distance."

When I reveal that Sheila has said to keep the change, his attitude shifts and he tries to calculate the price of dog food.

"She said that *I* can keep the change," I inform him, and he says that is just fine with him as long as I carry the damn stuff.

As it turns out we both cart the bag on the way back, my father gripping one end and me the other. In his other hand he clutches the bag containing our week's groceries: a couple of cans of Dinty Moore beef stew, a box of graham crackers, a can of Bluebird grapefruit juice, and a half-dozen eggs. Rather than buy a pack of Camels, he decides to purchase a pouch of Bugler cigarette tobacco, which is about half the price. This experiment proves to be disastrous because he cannot get the knack of rolling a butt that does not fall apart before reaching his lips.

"Goddamn stuff's no good. Who the hell could roll a smoke with this shit?" he growls, throwing his pathetic attempt on the floor and trying again with only slightly more success.

There is a used-car lot across the street from Sheila's with a HELP WANTED sign in the window. My father says he'll check it out tomorrow after a decent night's rest, adding that he really doesn't know much about hawking clunkers.

"The only thing I ever peddled was men's clothing and that was years ago. You have to know a little something about motors and mechanics to sell autos, but I can probably do it. I sure sold enough suits and sport jackets. Best salesman they had, and I was only a kid, maybe twenty-five."

Again he promises that if he's not able to find something to do to earn a few bucks to buy us a bus ticket, we'll try our luck at thumbing. The Barstow epic is never far from his thoughts when I raise the idea of hitchhiking, and I have to remind him of all the good luck we had catching rides before that. Yet he seems unable or unwilling to remember the better experiences.

"We came damn near being vulture meat," he says dolefully.

"It's only seven hundred miles to Albany," I say, and he comments that it's a long walk with holes in your shoes and that it will be a whole lot easier with our asses resting on a Greyhound bus seat.

When I drag the dog food to Sheila's I am invited into her apartment. With relief I discover that only the collie is there and he is thrilled by my presence. The others are outside in the yard, she points out.

"I have seven, all big males. You already met Wayland here. He's a real homebody. Rather stay inside with his mama than go out with the others. The big black one is a Great Dane," she says, pointing out the window.

"His name is Erik, like Erik the Red. I call him Erik the Great. He looks kinda scary but he's a real gentleman. You like your hair that way?" she asks, flicking her fingers through the strands that hang over my forehead. "Where'd you get this haircut? It's not very good. You could use a little pompadour like Elvis and Fabian. If you come by the salon tomorrow night, I'll do your hair for you. Would you like that? You have such a sweet face that the right hairstyle will make you really handsome."

"Sure," I answer as I attempt to dislodge Wayland's nose from between my legs.

"Stop that," orders Sheila, pulling at the dog's tail. "He's not a girl, you foolish thing. Don't let him bother you, hon. Animals will be animals sometimes."

When Wayland buries his snout in Sheila's lap, she chuckles and says that at least he's got the sex right this time.

During the night I'm awakened by the sound of a dog howling, and I go to the window to investigate the source of the racket. In the moonlight I see the Great Dane standing in the backyard with his huge head thrust skyward. This reminds me of the movie *The Hound of the Baskervilles* until Sheila walks naked across the patio and leads Erik inside.

Car Wash

THE NEXT MORNING I accompany my father to the used-car lot as he looks into the job opening advertised on a handwritten sign taped to the office window. As we approach, my father comments that he has seen better cars in a wreck.

We're greeted by a salesman as soon as we walk through the door, and he asks which of the beauties outside we're interested in. My father says he's there about the job, and the man replies that he'd be glad to help us out but that he doesn't get any commission for giving out information.

"Just kidding." He laughs and introduces himself as Jugger. "Mr. G.—it's short for Gariolli—is in the back. Go right down the Hall of the Damned, so named because all the pictures are of former Car Land employees. Mr. G.'s office is at the end . . . the dead end."

With this remark he twists his bushy mustache and says that if the job doesn't pan out he can make us a great deal on a 1949 Olds with low-mileage tires. My father tells me to wait while he inquires about the job, but then changes his mind and says to come with him.

"Maybe he has kids of his own," he reasons, and I figure that my presence may help him get the job.

There is a thick cloud of cigar smoke above the owner's disheveled desk. Behind him is a shelf laden with bowling trophies and an enlarged photo of him in a bowling shirt monogrammed

"Car Land." He is oblivious to our presence as we stand in the open doorway, and my father clears his throat to get his attention.

"What can I do for you?" he asks in a gruff voice.

His eyes look like small black buttons on a puffy pillow, and there are ashes up and down his white shirt. My father says he's there about the job, and Mr. G. says that if he can handle a bucket of water and live on seventy-five cents an hour, his quest for the perfect position is over.

"What you gotta do is wash and wax the junks out there and make them look better than they are so that we can unload them before they rot in place. If you can do that you're hired."

Before my father can answer, Mr. G. empties his nose into a Chock full o' Nuts coffee can by holding the bridge with his fingers and blowing with tremendous force.

"Yeah, I think I can handle that," says my father, winking at me, and the used-car dealer says he's got the job. My father takes out his wallet to offer his discharge and Social Security card as proof of identification and Mr. G. waves them away.

"You don't have to show me nothing," he says, pinching the slimy residue from his nostrils with his thumb and forefinger. "I don't care who you are as long as you didn't kill nobody, and then I don't care as long as you did it out of state. Can you start right away, like ten minutes ago?" he asks, and my father says he can.

"Good. There's some work pants in the closet across the hall. It's been pretty shitty weather lately and the cars out there don't look like they just come off the assembly line. Start with the ones up front first. Now I got work to do on this loan application."

In the corridor we bump into Jugger, who has apparently overheard the conversation.

"Congratulations. You've just joined the staff of Cincinnati's premier lemon farm. Don't scrub those heaps too hard or they'll fall apart before we can unload them. Did Mr. G. tell you our motto? 'We take you for a ride at Car Land.' Where you guys from?"

My father tells him we're from Albany and he says he's from the biggest little state in the United States: Rhode Island. Providence, to be exact. He used to have his own dealership there, he says, and hopes to get back to that part of the country soon. He then gulps from a bottle of Pepto-Bismol and explains that he's got the world's worst case of heartburn.

"Don't stand too close to me. When I burp I'm like a flame-thrower," he jokes, and takes another swig of the pink liquid. "This isn't a very good town for cheap eats and it sure as hell is no used-car-selling paradise," he laments, and my father remarks that he is pretty unimpressed with what he's seen of the place so far himself.

On my way out of the office, Jugger asks my name and tosses me a quarter, saying that I should buy a new Cadillac. My father instructs me not to wander too far, and I take my newfound wealth and head to the grocery store for a shopping adventure.

Lovely French Words

I SPEND MOST of the afternoon along the bank of the Ohio River watching colored people fish. When I hear a church bell chime five times I return home expecting to meet up with my father. He is not around when I arrive but Sheila sees me and says to come into her beauty salon.

"I believe you have an appointment, monsieur," she says, waving her hands like a pinwheel and grandly curtsying. "You know what *coiffure* means, hon? It's French for 'haircut' or 'styling.' That's why I call my place Sheila's Coiffures. Besides, I think it sounds real classy. You know what *merde* means in French? 'Poop.' Can you imagine that?"

Lavishly rolling her tongue, she repeats the word *merde*, and I think of Ryan's infatuation with foreign words.

"Imagine that. You can practically say anything in that beautiful language and it sounds elegant. *Merde*. Try saying it."

I take a stab at the French word and she applauds, saying that I *parlez-vous* better than she does. Meanwhile Erik the Great is sprawled out on the floor near the back of the salon, and Sheila encourages me to pet him, but when I approach he growls.

"Cut that out, you big bad boy. Whenever it's a full moon he gets real spooky. Last night all he wanted to do was bay at the moon. Maybe you heard him. I hope not, but he's pretty loud. None of the others get like that, only my big Danish pastry," she says, bending over and pulling his massive head up to her face. "That petite Parisian over there is Michel—that's French for Michael—and he's about to be transformed into a teenage heartthrob. So you behave, and don't give us any *merde.*"

Erik stares at me as Sheila holds his face in my direction, and the way she grips it causes his lips to spread apart, revealing two rows of gigantic fangs. This makes him look more ferocious than anything I have ever come face-to-face with and I plan to keep the full length of the room between us.

Sheila directs me to a salon chair and drapes a towel around my shoulders. The place has the same disgusting eggy odor that used to permeate the house when my mother gave herself a permanent. The Fabian look is right for me, she announces in a French accent, and I figure if she can make me look anything like him it's worth the humiliation of being tended to in a lady's barbershop.

It is around nine o'clock when my father appears, and I can tell he's been around alcohol.

"Where'd you get that pigeon on your head?" he asks with a taunting chuckle, referring to my new two-inch pompadour.

He is not drunk but he is feeling no pain, and when he flops into the overstuffed chair he looks more exhausted than intoxicated. I ask why he started drinking and he says that he hasn't started anything.

"Hit the sack. You're like an old broad," he complains. "Always crabbing over nothing. All I had was half a beer to be social to the guy I work with, for Christ's sake. Jugger's in AA and he can handle one or two drinks. So stop bitching at me. If you spent the day washing those rust buckets you'd need to unwind a little too."

Again I am roused in the middle of the night by a dog's howling, but this time I sense that it comes from within Sheila's apartment directly beneath our room and not from the backyard. The ruckus has awakened my father, who responds by munching on a graham cracker and smoking a cig. I don't let on that I'm awake, because I'm still perturbed at him and don't want to encourage his reminiscences about his prior life. Instead I just watch him standing at the window in only his T-shirt, searching for the hound from hell and mumbling a complaint about not having his Eveready.

Beastly Visions

GETTING GOING THE next morning is no easy challenge for my father, who looks more depleted than when he went to bed.

"Goddamn barking kept me up half the friggin' night," he complains, and asks if I heard it.

I tell him that I slept great, like a baby, just to compound his irritation. He is in the bathroom for what seems a prolonged amount of time and when he returns he combs his hair and inserts his false teeth after cleaning them with his shirttail. When he's about to leave for Car Land I warn him about drinking even half a beer, and he snaps back that he'll do whatever he damn well pleases. Before he shuts the door on his way out, he tells me not to worry and to stay close by.

Following a few strokes with my fingers to revitalize my drooping wave, it is where it was the night before. With nothing better to do I stroll back down to the Ohio River, where I find more people fishing than on the previous day. Later in the morning I head back to the rooming house for some graham crackers and on my way I meet a kid about my age who initiates a conversation. His name is Ian and he lives a couple of doors down from what he calls the dog lady's house. Not long into our talk he makes a revelation that completely shatters my view of Sheila.

"My dad says she does the thing with the big black dog."

"What thing?" I ask, and he indicates that she has sex with Erik the Great Dane.

"You know, she does this with him," he explains, illustrating his point by gyrating his hips and swooning. "She doesn't wear underpants either," he says, and I think that at least Sheila and I have that much in common.

We agree to meet later after he has lunch to toss a ball around and I go back to the room and devour several crackers while staring out the window at the backyard, where several of Sheila's furry friends are mulling about. As hard as I try to imagine her doing what Ian claims, I'm unable to formulate a clear picture of it.

When we meet up a couple of hours later he has more to say on the subject. According to his father, Sheila was treated for a severe bite on what he calls her hole.

"My dad has a friend who works at the hospital and he saw her come in for stitches right here on her hole," he says, pointing to his pelvic area. "My dad told my mom she had dog juice on it too."

For the balance of the afternoon we play catch and walk across a railroad bridge that joins Ohio with Kentucky. It excites me that I can actually hoof it from one state to another in a matter of minutes. When I observe to Ian, who is playing hooky from school, that we are walking from a Union state to a Confederate state, he says that most of the men from southern Ohio became rebs, not Yankees. I'm impressed with his knowledge and when I tell him so he remarks that history is his favorite subject in school, especially stuff about wars. When I tell him mine is geography, he asks me to name the capitals of several states, which I do with no problem. He then becomes an admirer of mine and we revel in our vast storehouses of historical and geographical knowledge.

During our river crossing I experience a sudden and unusual urge to move my bowels, so I squat on the tracks while Ian releases spit bombs into the murky brown water below. When I'm finished he remarks about the size of my stool, saying that he's never seen one so big and that it will probably derail the next train. I'm embarrassed and kind of proud at the same time.

"Must be a foot long. Looks like a giant slug. I think it's breathing," he jokes, poking at it with a stick, and when it falls between the tracks into the river he shouts, "Timber!" at the top of his lungs.

Sheila is sitting on the steps when we return and Ian suggests we see if she is wearing underpants by sitting on the step below her. Wayland the collie is with her and as soon as we sit down he mounts Ian's back and begins pumping his haunches against him. Ian shouts for the dog to get off and gives him a hearty shove that sends him back up the steps. Sheila laughs and says something about the dog always being in heat.

When she is not looking we steal a glimpse up her skirt and Ian's claim is confirmed. At first I am not sure what it is I'm looking at but then the expression on Ian's face makes it obvious. This is my first glimpse at a grown woman's genitals and they don't look very attractive to me. In fact the dark, fleshy area between her legs strikes me as rather repulsive—some crawly, damp alien thing in a 3-D sci-fi movie.

Again Wayland tries to have a go at Ian's back and this time he belts the dog in his snout, causing him to yelp. This angers Sheila, who tells him that it is very bad manners to be cruel to defenseless animals.

"He's just trying to play with you. You shouldn't be so mean," she says, and takes the dog inside.

"I told you she didn't wear underpants. My dad is right about her. She's queer," says Ian, and he makes a face to emphasize his disgust.

My father and Jugger are in our room when I return. Jugger has been evicted from his apartment for owing back rent and my father has invited him to sleep on the floor. Jugger has a plan that will get us back to Albany. It involves taking a car from the lot.

"I'll give Mr. G. a call when I get it to Providence, and he can have someone come and get the piece of junk. I'll drop you fellows off on the way."

We are slated to depart early the next day, but the immediate plan involves both of them attempting to dye the gray out of their hair with a box of Clairol women's coloring that I have lifted at the behest of my father from a shelf in Sheila's salon.

My father and Jugger will have a better shot at decent jobs if they look a few years younger, they conclude. While they apply the gook to their scalps in the bathroom, I entertain myself by chucking the small stones I've collected in my pocket at Sheila's furry Romeos in the backyard. My sharpshooter's eye allows me to land my projectiles on the flanks of the hounds, which causes them to leap in the air and run around in circles.

When my father and Jugger reenter the room, they are upset.

"Jesus Christ, look at us! What the hell was in that box you swiped?" snaps my father.

Although there is no longer any evidence of gray in their hair, there is a distinct pinkish tint emanating from their temples.

"Maybe you didn't do it right," I offer, on the verge of laughing.

"Who the hell is going to hire a guy who looks like a clown?" grumbles Jugger, tugging at his hair.

"The circus," I joke, and collapse on the bed in hysterics.

Jugger and my father spend most of the evening desperately trying to rid themselves of their crimson shame, but when we rise at the break of day they both look like they have little frizzy balls of cotton candy stuck to the sides of their head.

Last of Many Miles

WE BREAK DOWN just west of Youngstown and Jugger says that he should have known better than to think one of Car Land's shit boxes could have made it across the state line.

Eventually a guy in a battered Buick agrees to push us to the first garage, which turns out to be a used-car lot just inside the city limits.

"Maybe I can unload this clunker. I got the paperwork. Wait here—I'll see if I can make a deal," says Jugger, removing an envelope from the glove compartment.

In about half an hour he returns and reports that he's just sold Mr. G.'s rust bucket for $125 as is.

"When I get back to Providence I'll call and advise him where he can buy a great used car. That ought to piss off the son of a bitch," he says, swigging from his Pepto-Bismol bottle.

Jugger buys us tickets to Albany and at the last minute he decides to take a side trip to Pittsburgh to see his first ex-wife before going on to Rhode Island. Both our bus connections require about an hour wait. During this time Jugger and my father talk about a host of things, including Jugger's determination to get settled into a good job so that he can restore his broken-down wardrobe and get a decent apartment. With less than half an hour left before our buses are due to depart, Jugger excuses himself to go to the men's room, complaining about his heartburn. When he doesn't reappear as our buses are scheduled to load, my father decides to fetch him and I tag along. The rest room is empty and under a stall door we spot Jugger's scuffed loafers. My father taps on the stall door and calls his name but there is no response. As he is about to look under the door we hear an announcement that our bus is to leave momentarily, so my father abandons his efforts and directs me to our departure gate, where we climb onto our bus.

"Maybe he's dead," I say, and my father says he doubts it.

"Probably just snoozing or something. Pretty heavy sleeper. Corks off easily," he says unconvincingly, and I ask why he would go to sleep in the bathroom.

My father offers no answer as the bus rolls out of the depot, leaving Jugger's fate forever in question.

Before long we're back in the Empire State and my excitement about seeing my mother and sisters is gathering steam.

"Don't say much to your old lady, okay? Spare her the details. You know how upset she gets. Just say you had a good time. Tell her you went to school and always had enough to eat. If she asks where your things are, say they got stolen on the bus ride back," instructs my father nervously, and I wonder what I am going to tell her about not having any underpants on.

Central New York is flat and open and it reminds me of the Midwest a little, except it is greener and has more trees and the small towns we go through have narrower streets. I have left part of me on the sprawling plains and rolling prairies and I feel a tug of remorse that they are so far behind. This is not the land of cowpokes and roaming buffalo, even if it is the home of the Mohicans and other tribes. Somehow eastern Indians don't seem as legitimate to me as their western counterparts, who hunted and fought in the wide-open spaces of Nebraska, Kansas, and Oklahoma.

It is way past sunset when the bus descends the cobblestone avenue that leads from the New York State Capitol to the bank of the Hudson River and the bus depot. My father says it's too late to bother my mother, so with the extra money Jugger has given him we get a room in a run-down hotel nearby that has an abundance of cockroaches but no sign of bedbugs. When I attempt to pull down the shade, it rips in half and my father yells at me to leave things alone. He doesn't want to help pay to rebuild this flophouse, he says.

He is snoring before I drift off counting the flashes of a blue neon sign on the decrepit building across the street. It has blinked ——OC——TAILS at least a hundred times when sleep finally comes to me. Before my eyelids have dropped like a curtain at the end of a movie, I score the flickering scene beyond the grimy hotel window by joining it with a synchronized recitation of a passage from one of my favorite stories—" 'Robin . . . Robin . . . Robin Crusoe . . . poor Robin Crusoe! . . . Where are you . . . Robin Crusoe? . . . Where are you? . . . Where have you been?' "

Prodigal Returns

FROM TWO BLOCKS AWAY I recognize my mother's slender form. My sisters are not with her and this disappoints me, but I will see them soon enough.

Again my father coaches me on what to say and how to say it. He has become increasingly apprehensive since calling her, and he tensely scans our surroundings while pacing back and forth. We are meeting in front of the Wellington Hotel, where my father says he first met my mother.

"I was bellhopping there just before the war," he tells me. "She waitressed in the hotel coffee shop. They were good times, even if it was the end of the Depression. Everybody tipped great. Plenty of people had dough."

My mother catches sight of us and gallops in our direction. When she reaches us, she wraps her arms around me. Then she looks me up and down and comments about how thin I look.

"Don't worry—he's been getting three squares," says my father defensively, and my mother lets him have it with both barrels.

"How could you do this to him? He's skin and bones. Look at him. Are you sick, honey?" she asks, her face flush with anger and concern, and I say I'm fine, beginning to sense how much she has worried about me and how deeply she cares for me even though she let me go with my father.

There is no way she could love my sisters more than me, I determine, and I am as happy as I have been since reaching California.

"What a lousy thing to do to a child. You don't care about anyone but yourself. No normal person would drag their own kid around the country and let him go hungry. What is the matter with you? Where is your sense of decency? God, he's filthy," she fumes, attempting to rub some dirt from my forehead with a paper napkin and the spit she has applied to it. "His clothes! My God, how long have you been wearing these things? You couldn't even keep him clean, could you? You bastard!"

From out of nowhere a man in a dark suit and gray fedora approaches us. Nodding in my father's direction, he asks my mother if he is her ex-husband. With that he flashes a badge and my father looks as if he is about to vault over our heads.

"Yes, Officer," answers my mother, her face distorted with anxiety.

"Mr. Keith, if you'd come with me to the station, I'd like to ask you a few questions," says the policeman, reaching for my father's arm.

"What's the matter, for Christ's sake? He's my kid and I'm giving him back to his mother. Is that a crime?" responds my father desperately.

"Child abuse is a crime, sir," answers the officer, beginning to tug at my father's bony elbow.

My heart is pounding and I want to say something in my father's defense, but words can't get past the lump in my throat.

"What are you talking about? Does he look abused to you? Have I abused you, Butch? What's the matter with you people?" asks my father while resisting the officer's attempt to move him away.

In a surprising turnaround my mother tells the detective that everything is all right and that she isn't going to press charges after all. With that the officer gives her a disgusted look and releases my father.

"Have it your way, lady, but the kid don't look all that okay to me."

My mother tells him that I'm fine and things are going to be worked out. That I'm going back to live with her and won't be with my father anymore.

"It's your decision. You have to live with it," says the cop, and he trudges away.

"Jesus, that's a great way to welcome us back. You scared the shit out of the kid," says my father, holding on to my shoulder as if to steady himself.

All I can think of is how my mother actually came through with her threat to have my father arrested, and this serves as definitive proof of her true feelings about me. At the same time I am grateful that she has not had my father put in jail, and that act further deepens my estimation of her. I take her arm and hold it tightly.

"Do you have any idea at all, Curt, what it was like for me not knowing where he was?" she asks him. "If he was okay? If he was hurt or hungry? I cried myself to sleep at night worrying about it."

All of this is finally too much for my father and he starts to leave. Something in me sinks. The old familiar expression of dejection on his face gnaws at my heart and I begin to feel desperately sorry for him. Before he is more than a few steps away, he turns and gives me a sad smile and a wink. My eyes water up, and seeing this, my mother gives my hand a comforting squeeze.

"I'll see you soon, Butch. At least *you* don't hate me," he says, shooting my mother a look of triumph, and that is the last I see of him for quite some time.

Claudia and Pamela are thrilled to have me back and for the first few days they provide a receptive audience for my countless tales about life on the road and in Hollywood. In my exaggerated and grandiose accounts I have seen and talked with some of the biggest stars, and my sisters are enormously impressed.

The best part about being back is my mother's recently acquired twenty-one-inch Admiral television set. Her new friend and future husband, Chuck, is a *Collier's* magazine salesman and has won the set by topping all of his colleagues in signing up subscribers. He was in the navy at sixteen during the last days of the war and his ship saw action in the Pacific, but I'm not impressed, since he never actually got off it to fight on land like a real soldier.

"When you get old enough, join the military. They educate, feed, clothe, and house you, not to mention the travel. You can see the world for free. It's a good deal, especially during peacetime," he says, and it sounds pretty good to me, particularly the part about traveling the world.

Later, when my sisters are asleep and my mother and Chuck are in front of the TV in the living room, I imagine how great it would be to ship out to the South Pacific or the Arctic Circle, places far away from Albany, which has already lost most of its temporarily restored luster.

In my mother's house my sleep pitches and rolls from ceaseless motion. I run, ride, and even fly to countless wonderful places in my dreams, and my father is always there running, riding, and flying beside me.

Travel Companions

THE REMAINDER OF the summer passes slowly and as the start of school approaches I pray that my father will show up so that I can sell him on the idea of going to Florida. My interest in the tropics has peaked since watching the TV show *Adventures in Paradise,* and the thought of escaping the classroom and the boring routine of regular baths, Sunday masses, and early bedtimes with my mother makes me restless and irritable.

A month into the school term my father reappears. He is sober and standing in front of the Tri-City Mart, which is on my route home. My sisters choose to walk with their friends and I'm not about to hang out with a bunch of little girls. My old friends have formed new relationships and don't seem as interesting to me any-more anyway, so I go my own way alone most days, always on the lookout for my travel companion . . . my fellow adventurer.

As I approach where he is waiting, my father whistles and I re-turn our signal. We hug briefly and he says I look skinnier than when he last saw me.

"What's the matter, kiddo? Your old lady starving you? She never was much of a cook. Couldn't boil water," he says, and I report that I have gained five pounds, although I haven't actually weighed myself. "Yeah, in your hair," he jokes, patting my ever-ascending pompadour.

I tell him about my Florida idea, and he is not too enthusiastic initially but gradually comes around to my point of view, agreeing that he can easily get a job as a bellhop in Miami and maybe we should go after all. Besides, winter is just around the corner, he calculates, and he really doesn't look forward to the ice and snow, especially with his bursitis and bad back.

We settle on Friday as our departure date. I will meet him in the morning at the bus terminal, a place where I have spent considerable time since returning to Albany, and we will head south to the Sunshine State. He says he has enough dough from working at a hotel up in Saratoga to get us at least to Richmond, Virginia, and we shouldn't have much trouble catching a ride from there. The effects of the Mojave Desert have apparently faded, I happily conclude.

"Don't say anything to your mother. She'll have the cops after me again," he cautions, and for the next two days my mood is vastly improved as I anticipate hitting the road again.

Although I am careful not to breathe a word to my mother about taking off, I discuss the glories of life in the land of eternal summer with my sisters, making up a story about a boy who swims and plays with the dolphins and lives on coconuts he cuts from towering palm trees with his stiletto. Overhearing one of my tales, my mother remarks that I'm fast becoming a dreamer like my father.

WHEN FRIDAY MORNING ARRIVES, I toss my schoolbooks behind a clump of bushes and race to the bus station, my heart pounding with the anticipation of motion, my imagination already a thousand miles down the road.

MICHAEL C. KEITH, PhD, a member of the Communication faculty at Boston College and the author of over a dozen books, mostly on the subject of broadcast media, radio in particular, never graduated from high school. He enlisted in the army at seventeen, received his High School Equivalency Certificate, entered a program in radio announcing, and became a broadcaster. While raising his daughter as a single parent and working fulltime, he took advantage of the GI Bill and registered at a community college, eventually receiving his doctorate from the University of Rhode Island. His books include *Voices in the Purple Haze, Signals in the Air, and Sounds in the Dark.* The past Chair of Education for the Museum of Broadcast Communications, he and his wife live outside of Boston. His mother and sisters live nearby. Michael Keith's father died in 1982, still looking for the next better place.